HAWKER SIDDELEY
TRIDENT

Trident 1E G-AVYE at Wroughton in early 1986. This aircraft, which started life with Channel Airways and later operated with BEA and British Airways, was preserved by the Science Museum until she was replaced by Trident Three G-AWZM. Yankee Echo was broken up in 1989. *Author*

'Rotate!': Trident 3 G-AYVF climbs out of Hatfield's runway 06 in 1972. Victor Fox' should have carried the marks G-AWZY, but she was re-registered to avoid confusion with G-AWYZ.

Classic Civil Aircraft: 5

HAWKER SIDDELEY TRIDENT

MAX KINGSLEY-JONES

IAN ALLAN Publishing

First published 1993

ISBN 0 7110 2132 5

Published by Ian Allan Ltd,
Shepperton, Surrey;
and printed in Great Britain by
Ian Allan Printing Ltd,
Coombelands House,
Addlestone, Surrey KT15 1HY

**On 8 January 1963 Papa Bravo
arrived in Malta from Hatfield
via Nice. Based at Luqa,
Papa Bravo flew an average of
5½hr each day.** *via P. J. Cooper*

Contents

Front cover:
G-AVFI was used to unveil BEA's new corporate identity in August 1968. After demonstrating at the 1968 Farnborough Air Show, Fox' India was delivered to BEA in November 1968. She was amongst the first BA Trident 2s broken up at Heathrow during 1982. *BAe*

Back cover, top:
Channel Airways' first Trident 1E-140 'Continental Golden Jet' G-AVYB was delivered in May 1968. Following the airline's financial troubles she was acquired by BEA in December 1971 and spent several years with Northeast, before joining British Airways. Yankee Bravo was broken up at Heathrow in 1981, but her fuselage is used by the SAS at their training ground near Hereford. *BAe*

Back cover, bottom:
The summer of 1972, and no less than 8 BEA Tridents can be seen on the ground at Heathrow. *BAe*

Introduction

Now the Hawker Siddeley (née de Havilland) 121 Trident has been and gone in this everchanging world of commercial aviation, it is probably best remembered for the incredible amounts of noise it generated during take-off and climb, particularly by residents in the Heathrow locale. The noise problem was particularly contentious as the aircraft formed the backbone of BEA and British Airways' Heathrow operations for some 20 years. The sudden and complete demise of the type in Europe during the mid-1980s was no doubt welcomed by the aforementioned inhabitants, as well as many other dwellers near major European airports for that matter.

The Trident became a familiar sight around European airports for 20-odd years and as such aroused little interest, even from aviation enthusiasts. With only 117 aircraft sold to a total of nine customers, the Trident could hardly be called a commercial success.

Many a young BEA pilot cut his teeth on the Trident, and the aircraft's spacious flightdeck was to become 'the office' for thousands of British pilots during the 1960s, 70s and 80s. Crews had a warm respect for the aircraft and fondly nicknamed it 'Gripper' (to reflect its underpowered hunger for tarmac on take-off), 'Rodent' and 'Tripod'.

Never easy to fly, the Trident was however a pilot's aircraft with a very high cruising speed (it was one of the fastest subsonic airliners ever built) and fighter-like rate of roll. Although its take-off performance left something to be desired, to make a 'greaser' at 'the other end' would always be rewarded with a great feeling of achievement, particularly with the Trident 3.

However, the opportunities to land the Trident manually were relatively few and far between because the aircraft pioneered the development of 'Autoland'. As such the 'Tripod' proved to be a valuable asset to BEA and British Airways on its European network during the fog-bound winters of the 1960s, 70s and early 80s as well as the backbone of Shuttle and later Super Shuttle services for some 10 years.

What is fascinating about this apparently unremarkable aircraft is how it ended up achieving so little considering the huge potential that everyone saw for the design when first launched in the late 1950s. The political background to the birth (by Caesarian section) of the aircraft that was to become the Trident, has been painstakingly researched and the missed opportunities so easy to point out with the benefit of hindsight described. As well as charting the development and operation of

all production variants, a few amusing crew tales from the type's days of service with British Airways have been gathered together.

The author would like to record his thanks to the many people who freely contributed their time to assist him with the research and compilation of this book, namely: Chris Seymour for his assistance in reading the manuscript and making useful suggestions, Kingsley-Jones Studios (Windsor), Kevin Bowen and the Windsor Trident Collection (WTC), Mike Stroud, John Wegg, Airclaims Ltd, Robert Grundy (for his help with the monograph), Andy Mattocks (for giving the author the opportunity to 'fly' a Trident 3), BAe (Harry Holmes, Dave Wilkinson, Daryl Cott and Rob Morris), Mosquito Aircraft Museum, AIB Farnborough (Ken Smart), CAA, Peter Cooper and Peter Bish.

Thanks are also due to the 'posse' of former Trident pilots who provided much insight into what it was like to go to work with the 'Gripper', as well as confirming dates and details of last flights, namely: Mike Waldron, John Holland, Paul Heaver, Maurice Chick, Taff Thomas, Derek Woodward, Colin Rule, John Willats, Steve Hurst and John McIlwham.

Last but not least the author would like to thank his other half, Carmel, for her assistance on the manuscript, and for putting up with the Trident far beyond the call of duty!

Max Kingsley-Jones

The first Trident 3B, registered G-AWYZ, rotates from Hatfield. *BAe*

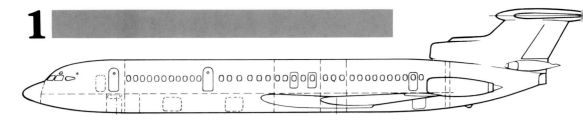

Origins

The pioneering development of commercial jet transport by Great Britain and in particular the de Havilland Aircraft Company in the 1940s and 1950s, has already been chronicled in much detail elsewhere. Indeed, the company was to kickstart the world into the new era of jet transportation when it flew the Comet prototype from Hatfield on 27 July 1949, the four-engined jet aircraft being the world's first purpose-built jet airliner to fly.

The Comet in its original guise (as delivered to BOAC in 1951-52) was promoted as a long range aircraft, but in fact it had the same maximum gross weight as the Trident when that programme was launched in August 1959, and a similar range (1,500 miles). The aircraft's cruising speed was significantly lower than the Trident, and payload was about half that of the new aircraft, which illustrated the extent to which the de Havilland jet aircraft design had progressed over the decade.

Interestingly, some of de Havilland's pre-Comet studies for a jet airliner envisaged a design based on the Vampire fighter airframe powered by three jet engines, all of which were buried in the rear fuselage, the centre one below the tail. The aircraft was, however, only expected to have accommodation for six passengers, but did offer London-New York range.

Despite the false start that the original Comet experienced with its untimely withdrawal from airline operations in April 1954, the world's aircraft manufacturers needed no further prompting to develop their own jet transports. The four-engined Avro Canada C102 Jetliner, which flew just two weeks after the first Comet, was, unlike the British design, envisaged from the start for short to medium range intercity routes and was effectively set to become the world's first 'regional jet airliner'. Unfortunately, Avro was forced to shelve the design by the Canadian Government in favour of the development of military jets.

Boeing quickly developed the 707 intercontinental jet from the Dash Eighty prototype, whilst McDonnell Douglas followed its long line of piston 'DCs' with the four-jet DC-8. By the second half of the 1950s de Havilland had overcome the Comet's teething problems and the type was about to re-enter service with BOAC in an enlarged, re-engined, longer range form, known as the Comet 4. The Comet and the 707 inaugurated transatlantic jet services during the autumn of 1958 with BOAC and Pan American respectively.

With the market apparently now saturated with four-engined long range jetliners, Convair developed a smaller high speed subsonic jet airliner, the 880, which offered less capacity than the Boeing and Douglas products but was capable of cruising at over 600mph, making it the fastest jet transport of its day and considerably faster than its rivals. Unfortunately for Convair, the speed gimmick did not really catch on.

During 1957 de Havilland began finalising plans for a short range, higher capacity version of the Comet 4, which eventually received a launch order from BEA in the form of the Comet 4B in August 1957.

In the meantime, the French manufacturer Sud Aviation had developed the world's first true short range jet airliner in the form of the twin-engined SE210 Caravelle. The aircraft had been launched into production in 1953 and the prototype made its first flight from Toulouse on 27 May 1955. Although initially proposed as a trijet with its centre engine buried in the tail, the aircraft evolved as a twin-engined design powered (initially) by two 10,000lb thrust Rolls-Royce Avon turbojets. The launch customer Air France placed orders for 12 in February 1956 to operate on its European regional routes, and the aircraft entered revenue service with the airline in April 1959. Scandinavian Airlines System (SAS) became the first export customer for the type when it ordered six, plus 19 options, in June 1957.

Despite the snowballing development of the jet transports in both the short and long range markets, Britain's European airline British European Airways (BEA) apparently felt that propeller turbine power

power (turboprop) was the way to go on the shorter routes rather than pure jet. Having successfully introduced the 50-seat turboprop Vickers Viscount into regular service in April 1953, the following year BEA issued a detailed specification for a larger turboprop-powered successor, which was to lead to the development of the Vickers Vanguard. The airline placed launch orders for the type on 20 July 1956 and aimed to introduce its first 114-139 seat Vanguards on its European routes during 1960.

However, the advent of a European short haul jet aircraft in the form of the Caravelle led BEA to reconsider its options. It could now anticipate Air France having a jet competing on its routes by the turn of the decade, before its turboprop Vanguards were due to come on line. Indeed, the Caravelle had made swift progress, picking up orders from several key European airlines, and BEA may have begun to ponder whether its new Vanguards would be obsolete before they started working on its European network.

Therefore in July 1956, the same month that it finalised its contract for the Vanguard and just four months after Air France placed its Caravelle order, BEA issued its requirement for a 100-seat 600mph-plus jet airliner capable of carrying a payload of up to 19,000lb (70 first class passengers) out of 6,000ft runways over 1,000-mile sectors. The aircraft was to be able to offer the best seat-mile costs over ranges from 500-1,000nm and be available to enter service by 1964. Significantly, BEA's requirement stated that its new jet should be faster than the Caravelle. BEA also wanted its new jet to have 'more than two engines' with a preference expressed for rear-mounting.

In spite of this requirement, at the end of 1956 the BEA Chairman Lord Douglas stated that the core of the airline's fleet would continue to be with the British turboprop, although he conceded that the company could need to acquire a few jets to counter the competition. Less than nine months later, the Chairman stated 'we were at one time hoping to go on indefinitely with turboprops,' and now seemed resigned to the fact that it was going to have to follow its fellow European airlines into acquiring jets.

Apparently concerned at the sudden interest in a jet rather than turbine-powered regional airliner, Vickers itself undertook studies of a trijet version of the Vanguard, dubbed the 'Vanjet'. The aircraft featured a new swept wing and three Rolls-Royce Avons mounted on the rear fuselage, two in pods either side and the third buried in the tail. The crucifix tailplane layout was borrowed from the Caravelle. Vickers used a novel installation for its central engine, with its air intake located on the top of the fuselage feeding the engine by way of an 'S'-shaped intake duct. The installation was similar to

that of the Martin XB-51 light bomber of 1949 and the proposed trijet Caravelle.

The Vanjet was effectively Vickers' insurance against the loss of the BEA and Trans Canada Airlines launch orders for the Vanguard, in the event of the two airlines rethinking their selection of the turboprop. In the end the orders remained, and so the Vanjet failed to materialise. However, the Vanjet's design was to be influential in other manufacturers' proposals for the BEA requirement.

De Havilland proposals that eventually led to its submission of the Model 121 to BEA can be traced back to late 1956. Following the BEA requirement of July 1956, and a requirement by BOAC for a new long range jet, de Havilland conceived the DH118 in the autumn 1956, although this proposal was aimed primarily at the BOAC requirement. The DH118 was in fact a development of the proposed Comet 5, itself a derivative of the Comet 4, with four pod-mounted Rolls-Royce Conway turbofans and capable of cruising at around 550mph. At the end of 1956, BOAC was believed to be in negotiation with de Havilland for the purchase of up to 15 DH118s.

By the end of the year the de Havilland proposal had developed into the DH119 powered by four Rolls-Royce RA29 Avons and aimed more at BEA's requirement. The engine installation on the '119 was behind the rear wing spars with air intakes below the wings and this layout was carried over to its successor, the DH120 which aimed at satisfying both corporations' requirements. The '120 was proposed with either the four Rolls-Royce RA29 Avons of the DH119, or RB140s (scaled down Conways).

However, the '119 and the ambidextrous '120 satisfied neither BOAC nor BEA, the former already favouring Vickers' scaled up Vanjet, the VC-10, whilst the '120 was too big for the latter. De Havilland therefore decided to aim directly at BEA's requirement and conceived the Model 121 in May 1957.

Initially, the 121 (de Havilland's 121st design) was proposed as a 79-seat 126,000lb gross weight aircraft powered by either three or four 'bypass jets' in the 8,000-12,000lb thrust class. De Havilland however favoured the trijet design which featured three 12,130lb thrust RA29 Avons with the Caravelle/Vanjet-inspired tail layout, albeit with the tailplane positioned below the central engine. Both designs envisaged fully powered flying controls.

The proposed aircraft had an overall length of 110ft 4in, and a wingspan of 111ft. Wheel track was 19ft 4in and wheel base 45ft 7in. A conventional undercarriage layout was adopted, with a twin nosewheel unit and four-wheel bogey main units.

The centre engine was positioned atop the rear fuselage, fed by a straight-through air intake. The four-engined proposal featured four 8,550lb thrust

Illustration of the de Havilland DH121 as first proposed to BEA in May 1957. Note the straight-through air intake and low-set tail. *Kevin Bowen/WTC*

Rolls-Royce RB140 engines mounted in paired pods on the rear fuselage (as with the VC-10). A further proposed trijet derivative featured the proposed Rolls-Royce RB141 engine rated at 11,660lb thrust each. The aircraft was expected to have a cruising speed of 605mph at 24,000ft, and a maximum range of 1,140 miles. It is interesting that in the proposal put to BEA, de Havilland stated that it considered the aircraft might be the last subsonic short range jet to be designed in Great Britain.

As initially proposed, the '121 featured not one but two ventral airstairs (something never fitted on the production aircraft), one of which was situated conventionally in the rear fuselage; however the other installation was far more novel. Positioned in the forward fuselage just behind the flightdeck, the airstair would be lowered from the nose gear bay through which passengers would enter and exit.

The number of engines for the new short haul jet was to be one of the biggest behind-the-scenes technical debates of the year. The BEA requirement for 'more than two engines' had effectively ruled out a twin. The major airlines in the United States had also stated that they were not interested in anything less than three engines for those sort of ranges.

The preference, and later the decision, to opt for 'less than four engines' boiled

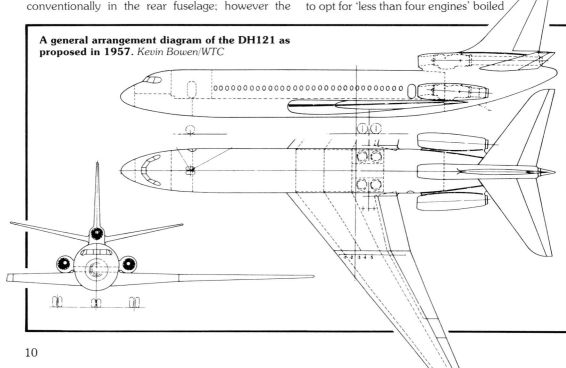

A general arrangement diagram of the DH121 as proposed in 1957. *Kevin Bowen/WTC*

down to direct operating costs (DOCs). Studies carried out by Rolls-Royce and de Havilland showed that a four-engined aircraft would have between 3% and 5% higher DOCs. Similarly, a twinjet design capable of 600mph would require a higher aspect ratio wing, and would have been significantly overpowered in the cruise, as its total available thrust would have to be able to cope with engine-out take-off requirements.

By July 1957, de Havilland's '121 proposal had been re-thought and featured a gross weight of 107,000lb with three 10,400lb thrust Rolls-Royce RB-140-141 bypass engines, later called Medways, selected for the powerplant. As the DH121's design was refined, a T-tail arrangement was adopted with the tailplane being moved to the top of the fin. At the same time the Vanjet's buried central engine and 'S'-shaped intake duct layout was incorporated.

During 1957 two other manufacturers submitted designs to BEA to meet its future short haul jet needs. Bristol proposed its Model 200 which in its final form was similar in layout to the 121 with three (initially four) engines mounted on the rear fuselage, the central one fed by an 'S'-duct.

Manchester's A.V. Roe & Co (known simply as Avro) had in fact been the first company publicly to reveal its proposals for a short range jet for BEA. In the July 1957 edition of *Avro News*, the company's Managing Director Sir Roy Dobson referred to its proposal as a 'determined attempt to enter the civil airliner markets'. He also stated that the company could not afford to 'underestimate the opposition' and emphasised the fact that Avro would be 'risking

many millions of our own money in this venture, so it had better be successful...'

Avro put forward the Model 740 which was developed from some earlier work carried out by Armstrong Whitworth. Powered by three Olympus 551s, the design differed somewhat from the de Havilland and Bristol offerings, featuring a more novel three-engined layout. The central engine was mounted in a pod on top of the fuselage between two V-fin tailplanes. The other two engines were in pods on the rear fuselage as with the DH121 and Bristol 200. Significantly, unlike the other two companies that had submitted proposals, right from the start Avro was offering to finance the development of its project (estimated to be some £17-£20 million) by recouping its investment through export orders.

In August 1957, BEA satisfied its immediate jet requirement by announcing that it would order six de Havilland Comet 4Bs, a short range, higher capacity development of the intercontinental Comet 4, for delivery from the end of 1959. However, this was an interim measure and it would appear that at the same time BEA selected the DH121 over the Bristol 200 and Avro 740 for its longer term requirements.

Up until this point the Bristol 200 was believed to have been BEA's favoured design. However, as far back as July 1957, de Havilland had promoted the DH121 as a supplement as well as an eventual replacement for BEA's anticipated fleet of Comet 4Bs. It would seem that BEA's interim requirement for jets, satisfied by the Comets, swayed its preference away from the Bristol offering towards the de

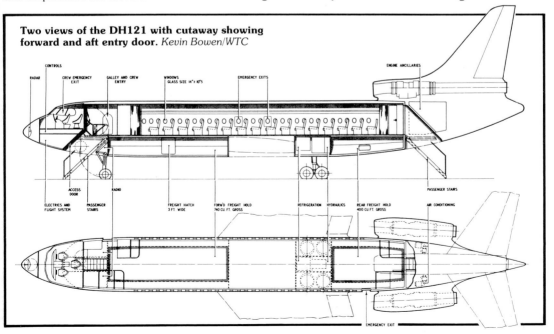

Two views of the DH121 with cutaway showing forward and aft entry door. *Kevin Bowen/WTC*

The DH121 as proposed during 1958, with its T-tail layout and S-shaped air intake duct feeding the No 2 engine which was buried in the tail. Although the design still had several years of evolution — and more significantly, interfering to come — the shape that was to become the silhouette of the ubiquitous Trident is clearly evident. *BAe*

Havilland 121. At this time, BEA wanted to start taking delivery of its all-new jets before the end of 1962.

Up until the time BEA approached the Treasury for the necessary financial support to launch its jet airliner project, apparently it had been assumed that the government would be prepared to support the project financially. As such, of the three offerings only Avro's proposal was planned to be financed privately. It therefore came as a bit of a shock when Mr Harold Watkinson, Minister of Transport, announced on 9 December 1957 at the BIATA (British Independent Air Transport Association) annual dinner that the new trijet would have to be financed privately.

It was during 1957 that the then Conservative government began to encourage its policy of combining the many British aircraft manufacturers into larger, less numerous groupings. This was achieved by using its control of the state airlines to push through its belief that collaboration was the answer to future projects. As the government was to provide BEA with the finances for its new fleet in the form of a loan, the order would have to be subject to its approval.

Neither Bristol nor de Havilland could finance their projects individually and so the turn of the year saw some frantic rejigging as various new proposals were put to the Minister. De Havilland proposed a consortium to BEA to build the '121, which it would lead (building the fuselage) and would include Hunting, Fairey and its rival Bristol who would be responsible for building the wings. Bristol was obviously not keen on playing second fiddle to de Havilland, and on 27 December 1957 announced that it was joining forces with Hawker Siddeley to produce the '200, with the shareholding split 35:65 per cent respectively. This effectively eliminated the Avro offering, as the company was a division of the Hawker Siddeley Group (and had been since the group was formed in 1935). The plan was that the Bristol-Hawker Siddeley company

would be formed 'to undertake a jet airliner to BEA specifications'.

The chairman of the Bristol-Hawker Siddeley joint venture, whose combined assets exceeded £200 million, was Sir Frank Spriggs, Managing Director of Hawker Siddeley Group. Other directors included Avro Managing Director Sir Roy Dobson, Sir Reginald Verdon Smith, Chairman and joint MD of Bristol, and Short Brothers/Bristol Chairman, Rear-Admiral Sir Matthew Slattery.

In a statement issued in January 1958 the consortium stated that 'the new company operating with the full support of the parent companies, will employ the strongest resources of the two parent companies in engineering, manufacture and sales, so as to develop and produce the aircraft as rapidly as possible, and on a scale to enable it to be offered in world markets at dates, times and prices which will be internationally competitive. To this end the new company will hold the contract, will have a direct relationship with BEA and other customers on all aspects of the project, and will be responsible for specification, airworthiness, planning and progressing, sales, engineering and promotion.'

It was planned to divide design and production to enable the civil aviation experience of Bristol and the high subsonic speed experience of Hawker Siddeley to be deployed to the best advantage. There had been suggestions that BEA's previous selection of the de Havilland design over the Bristol 200 was unlikely to have been on technical preference as it was purported that there was little to choose between them at this early stage. BEA's favouring of the de Havilland 121 was more likely to do with the commercial continuity that the company could offer in jet airliner design, having already built and delivered the Comet. This would explain the emphasis made in the Bristol-Hawker Siddeley statement over the consortium members' experience in their relevant fields of aviation.

The creation of the Bristol 200 consortium was to put governmental pressure on BEA to change

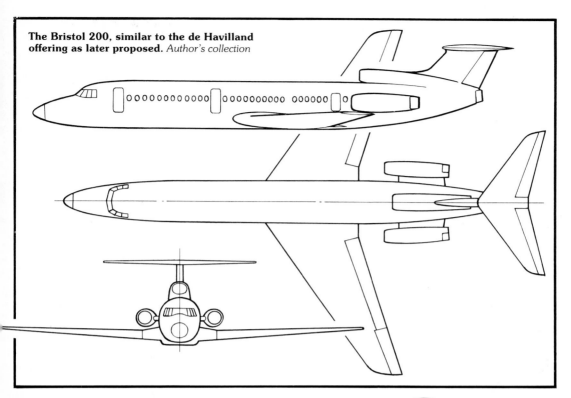

The Bristol 200, similar to the de Havilland offering as later proposed. *Author's collection*

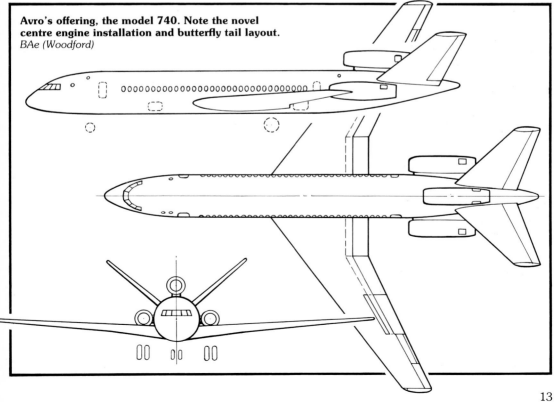

Avro's offering, the model 740. Note the novel centre engine installation and butterfly tail layout. *BAe (Woodford)*

direction away from the '121 as it awaited final government approval for its purchase of 24 DH121s. The Corporation's board met on the afternoon of Friday 3 January 1958 to deliberate on its selection on the '121 over the newly proposed Bristol-Hawker Siddeley consortium's proposal.

In January 1958, Bristol-Hawker Siddeley went public with its Bristol 200 design, and sent a sales team to the US to enter discussions with Pan American over a possible order. This proved to be an effective attempt to steal the limelight from the DH121 by Bristol. There were even suggestions that the Bristol-Hawker Siddeley programme would go ahead with or without the BEA order, should they secure '20, 30 or 40' orders. As then proposed, the Bristol 200 had an overall length of 121ft 6in, a wingspan of 91ft and the proposed powerplants were 'three turbojets in the 13,000lb thrust class' (assumed to be the Rolls-Royce RB141s). The aircraft had a range with its maximum passenger load (100 passengers) of 1,700st miles, a maximum gross weight of 120,000lb and a maximum payload of 21,000lb.

De Havilland meanwhile had finalised its own amalgamation plans, *sans* Bristol, and called it the Aircraft Manufacturing Company (Airco). Revealed in January 1958, Airco was the revival of an old name that existed during World War 1 in which Sir Geoffrey de Havilland was the chief designer and which built the de Havilland DH1 to DH18. De Havilland was to have a 67.5% shareholding with Hunting 22.5% and Fairey 10%, with the members represented on the board by four, two and one directors respectively. Handley Page had offered technical experience using its experience with high speed aircraft and tail design. Saunders-Roe was also pencilled in for sub-contract work on the '121. Rolls-Royce was to be technically responsible for the development of the powerplant (RB141) for the DH121 as well as its installation.

The stumbling block over the selection of the source for BEA's new airliner seemed to be based upon fears that the de Havilland was not as strong in terms of size, assets and production capacity as the rival Bristol-Hawker Siddeley consortium, which through the Hawker Siddeley Group included Avro, Amstrong Whitworth, Gloster and Hawker. Therefore, although BEA favoured the de Havilland proposal for the reasons already suggested, the government apparently preferred the stronger Bristol consortium.

Hence the creation of the Airco consortium, which was primarily aimed at swinging government support away from the strong Bristol-Hawker Siddeley consortium to BEA's preference, the de Havilland group. At the end of January 1958, de Havilland went on record to state that 'the three Airco companies concerned have more than adequate financial resources to carry the risk of selling or not selling the DH121, assuming that the BEA order is for 20 to 25 aircraft'.

Bristol-Hawker Siddeley had been suggesting that de Havilland's negotiations for the order had involved discussion over progress payments that could amount to £10 million by the time of first deliveries, and it was further implied that this could be lost should the programme fail.

Following the completion of the DH121's consortium, the final de Havilland proposal was put to the Minister of Supply on 23 January 1958. In the parliamentary civil aviation debate on 27 January 1958, Harold Watkinson stated 'the history of BEA's attitude was that to begin with, it favoured the Bristol concept, but after discussion and technical examination the final decision was in favour of the de Havilland design. I do not think that there is now any aircraft manufacturer who has not had a chance to associate himself with this order if he wants to. The final detailed proposals from the de Havilland group reached my Right Honourable friend and myself only this morning. They are being urgently examined.'

In a House of Commons statement issued on 10 February, the Minister of Supply, Aubrey Jones, summed up the purpose of his approach to the problem of the BEA order. Firstly he wished to ensure that the project would not involve financial liabilities on his department, partly because such liabilities had been heavy in the past, and partly because it was healthier for the industry to be more self-reliant. De Havilland's first proposal required government financial contribution. The proposal of 19 December had promised private financing among the other contractors with reservations about the volume of other Ministry contracts. However, the latest proposals were being considered to make sure that his department was protected against contingent liabilities. The alignment of home demand with potential foreign demand was also being looked at.

The controversy seemed to be sown up when, on 12 February 1958, the Ministry of Transport and Civil Aviation (MTCA) announced that BEA was to begin final negotiations with Airco and Rolls-Royce over the acquisition of 24 DH121s (plus 12 options). A Letter of Intent was signed, with deliveries scheduled to begin in early 1964.

The government also stated however that it would 'wish to be satisfied that the whole project will be developed and manufactured as a private venture by the companies concerned'.

During 1958, BEA approached Smiths Industries and asked the company to develop an all-weather flight control system for its new jet airliner; the plan being that the aircraft would eventually be able to land automatically in all weathers, including the dense fog which was a feature of smoggy Europe in the 1950s.

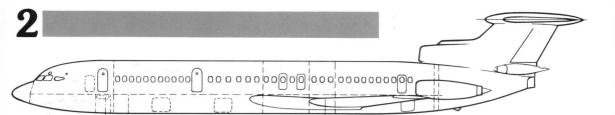

2

For Bigger, For Smaller...

Final MTCA (Ministry of Transport and Civil Aviation) approval for BEA's Airco 121 order was announced in the House of Commons by the Minsister of Transport, Harold Watkinson, on 1 August 1958. The Minister had written to Lord Douglas on 30 July advising him that the government agreed to the airline concluding the contract with de Havilland. The order for 24 aircraft was valued at £29m including spares and the magazine *Flight* estimated the unit cost of the DH121, allowing for spares, to be £1m. Delivery was expected between 1964 and 1966.

With all the contentions over the order now seemingly out of the way, and government approval awarded, the final contract signing could reasonably have been anticipated within a fairly short period. Indeed, the Airco partners had made considerable progress with the preliminary design of BEA's new short haul jet. However, the circumstances up to the final contract signing were not to be quite as straightforward as would have been hoped.

Despite its selection by BEA, de Havilland elected to keep the exact details of its DH121 design under wraps and, compared to Bristol, released very little information for the 1958 Farnborough Air Show in September.

Whilst Bristol supplied information about the '200's gross weight (120,000lb), engines (Bristol Olympus or a US version of the engine — Curtis Wright Zephyr — for the US market), dimensions (span 91ft, length 121ft 6in) and performance (21,000lb payload over 1,000 miles at 600mph cruise), the Airco partners simply displayed models of the DH121 with no real details. All that was known was that the aircraft would be powered by three 12,000lb thrust Rolls-Royce RB141s and would have a gross weight in the region of 120,000lb. Rolls-Royce had stated that the new engine would have 'a specific fuel consumption and a noise level, without suppressors, much lower than any existing engine of comparable thrust'.

A specification booklet thought to have been published during 1958, describing de Havilland's definitive DH121, which was presumably not in the public domain, revealed that the aircraft had an overall length of 126ft 8in (fuselage length — 117ft 3in), a wingspan of 107ft with an area of 1,920sqft and 35-degree sweep. The aircraft had a design gross weight of 122,500lb, a relatively high landing weight of 117,000lb (to allow multi-sector operations without refuelling) and a payload of 23,000lb.

The aircraft featured a novel undercarriage installation in that the nose gear was offset to port by 24in and retracted sideways to make more economical use of the underfloor space and allow a longer cargo hold. It also enabled a large electrical bay to be installed under the flightdeck. The main gear had a four-wheel bogey layout that was designed to retract conventionally into the wing centre section.

Powerplant was the Rolls-Royce RB141 turbojet engine with thrust reversers fitted to the outboard engines. The centre engine was located aft of the primary structure. The DH121's primary structure was designed for an initial 10-year crack-free life with failsafe characteristics.

The DH121 was designed to be equipped with an onboard Auxiliary Power Unit (APU) to provide an independent source for the air conditioning and engine start. The aircraft was to have fully powered flying controls without manual revision, with each engine driving an independent hydraulic pump and electrical generator to give triple redundancy.

Two passenger doors were provided on the port side, one forward and one just ahead of the wing. A service door/emergency exit was fitted opposite both, plus one additional exit aft of the wing on the starboard side. The aircraft was equipped with two overwing exits on each side of the fuselage.

The flightdeck was designed for operation by 'Captain, first officer and a third crew member' with a removable seat for one supernumerary crew. The design of the flightdeck would enable the third crew member to face forward rather than sideways at critical times. Compared to the Comet, visibility from the flightdeck was vastly improved with nine large main window panels and four eyebrow windows.

The fuselage had an outside diameter of 12ft 1.5in (11ft 5in internal) and was capable of seating up to 111 passengers in a single class layout at 34in pitch six-abreast. Alternatively, a two-class layout proposed 15 first class seats (38in pitch five-abreast) and 78 economy seats for a total of 93.

Having been beaten by de Havilland, Bristol did not lie down, but in fact developed a smaller short haul jet proposal, the 58-seat Model 205, aimed at the Viscount/Convair 440 replacement category. Powered by four 5,000lb thrust Bristol Orpheus jets the aircraft was designed to operate over ranges of 200 to 1,400 miles. During 1959 it began urging the new proposal on BEA. Although this project in the end came to nought, it may have had some bearing on the corporation's thinking, and at that time it was still in negotiation with Airco over the DH121 purchase.

By early 1959 the DH121 had a gross weight of around 123,000lb and maximum seating for 111 passengers. Power from the RB141 Medway engine was 12,000lb with 14,000lb on the horizon. Airco also envisaged growth versions of the 121 having gross weights of 140,000-150,000lb. De Havilland market studies suggested sales of as many as 550 aircraft in that category by 1965.

However, by March 1959, following a dip in passenger growth, BEA was convinced that the '121 had grown too much and felt that it could not warrant the introduction of such a large aircraft on to its network in the near future. BEA believed that the falter in traffic growth was an indication that the industry was not likely to grow in the short term anywhere as near as much as had been imagined in the preceding years. As such it was felt that the growth would not allow the fleet of 24 large DH121s to be accommodated even if it was assumed that all the airline's Viscounts were disposed of, and given the fact that the corporation had another high capacity aircraft, the Vanguard, also on order.

It appeared that on the surface, de Havilland was of a similar opinion to BEA regarding the size of its aircraft, and fully supported the request by its customer. However, studies carried out by some of the Airco analysts revealed that, if anything, the DH121 was somewhat smaller than ideal. Apparently a false document was created by the manufacturer supporting the BEA opinion and contravening its own market studies. Certain analysts in the company felt strongly about the whitewash and were almost sacked for refusing to sign the fabricated document.

Predictably the pressure from BEA saw the decision taken to scale the aircraft down to be a 97-seater powered by three all-new 10,100lb thrust turbofan engines to be produced by Rolls-Royce. Designated the RB163, this engine was later to be named the Spey and would go on to power a number of different types of aircraft.

The apparent ease with which de Havilland and its partners backed down over its plans for the DH121 can be understood if one remembers that at the time there were still a number of potential alternative suppliers that BEA could turn to, to get its own way, and de Havilland desperately wanted to finalise its hard-fought-for contract.

The press reported that de Havilland had spent some £800,000 on DH121 development to date and it was questioned as to how the wasted portion of this sum was to be recovered. It was also assumed that the unit cost of the new smaller aircraft would be reduced from the original 'sticker price' of £1.05m.

The new aircraft retained the original '121's fuselage cross-section, although it was shortened by about 13ft and all the flying surfaces were scaled down with wing area reduced by about 30 per cent. Wingspan was reduced by about 17ft to 89ft 10in and its area to 1,350sq ft, although the 35-degree wing sweep was retained. Maximum gross weight was down to 105,000lb, whilst Maximum Landing Weight (MLW) was 100,000lb (ie, 95 per cent of Maximum Take-Off Weight (MTOW)).

At the time, the full long term consequences of the decision to shrink the '121 at BEA's request

The DH121 as it was being proposed just before the scaling down of the design. In this form with its Medway engines and large wing, the aircraft was set to become a world beater. *BAe*

16

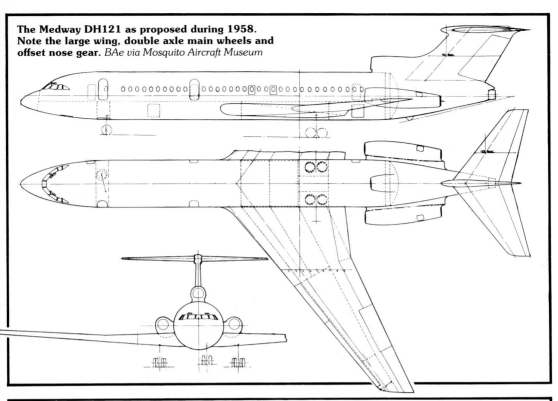

The Medway DH121 as proposed during 1958. Note the large wing, double axle main wheels and offset nose gear. *BAe via Mosquito Aircraft Museum*

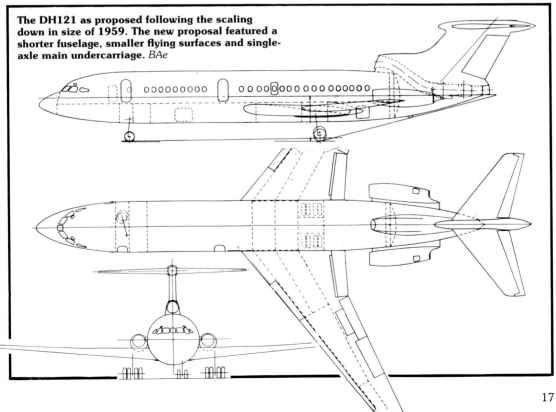

The DH121 as proposed following the scaling down in size of 1959. The new proposal featured a shorter fuselage, smaller flying surfaces and single-axle main undercarriage. *BAe*

After the size shuffle, BEA was finally ready to sign a contract with de Havilland for its new short haul jet. This occurred on 12 August 1959 and a signing ceremony took place at BEA's headquarters at Keyline House. Here Sir Aubrey Burke, Managing Director of Airco (left) is pictured shaking hands with Mr Anthony Milward, Chief Executive of BEA, after signing the £28 million contract for 24 DH121s plus 12 options. A model of the 121 is displayed in the foreground. *BAe*

were apparently not appreciated by most, and the general feeling even amongst the press seemed to be that it was for the best. It was not until the mid 1960s that the huge missed opportunities that had resulted from the shrink were fully recognised and opinion changed (with the benefit of hindsight) to a feeling of annoyance at the shortsightedness on the part of BEA and de Havilland.

BEA finally signed a purchase contract with Airco on 12 August, 1959 for 24 plus 12 options valued at £28m. Attending the signing ceremony at BEA's headquarters at Keyline House, Ruislip, were Anthony Milward, Chief Executive of BEA and Sir Aubrey Burke, Managing Director of the Airco consortium.

Commenting on the order Mr Milward confirmed that 12 DH121s remained on option adding 'we hope it won't end there'. Break-even sales for the DH121 were said to be 100 aircraft. He described the DH121 being as 'as near to a Viscount replacement as has yet been seen'. Sir Aubrey Burke stated that 'I don't suppose anyone will do (a short haul jet) any quicker', and also mentioned 'the very great co-operation that has been received from Rolls-Royce'.

Production of the first machine had in fact commenced on 29 July 1959 and the first flight of the DH121 was set for December 1961 with deliveries to BEA scheduled to take place in three batches between late 1963 and 1966.

Just one month after the revamped 'shrunk' DH121 finally received its launch order, Boeing, which was also working on a short to medium range airliner under the project name 727, finalised its design. What it had decided upon was a 140,000lb 130-seat trijet powered by three 13,000lb thrust engines — exactly what the de

Havilland designers had on the drawing board in early 1959 when BEA demanded its rethink.

Following a visit to the US by BEA's Chairman Lord Douglas, there was for a time the possibility of collaboration with Boeing on the '121. He felt that as both the British company and the US manufacturer were studying trijet designs (the former at this stage significantly further along the development cycle), that it would make sense if they got together.

In early 1960 Boeing was naïvely invited to make a very close inspection of de Havilland's trijet research and the '121's design and performance. Indeed, it seemed that de Havilland apparently enjoyed showing the competition its design studies as Convair officials were also invited to study the DH121. The compliment was returned by Boeing in May 1960 and four de Havilland engineers — C. T. Wilkins (chief designer), D. R. Newman (chief technician), John Wimpenny (senior aerodynamicist) and Peter Hall (sales manager) — visited Seattle. However, little or nothing of the US manufacturer's plans were revealed to de Havilland.

The insight it had into de Havilland's trijet studies certainly influenced Boeing's design formats on certain aspects of the 727, and when the aircraft was formally launched at the end of 1961 (to the tune of 80 orders from Eastern and United), it bore a striking resemblance to the DH121. However, the first 727 was not expected to fly until early 1963, apparently giving the DH121 at least a year's head start on its rival.

Shortly after the finalising of the BEA contract, the first full details of the 'new' DH121 were revealed. Maximum speed was 606mph (Mach 0.875 at 25,000ft) whilst its economical cruise speed of 585mph at 32,000ft (Mach 0.87) was faster than any other commercial aircraft then in existence. At its economical cruise speed/height the DH121 could carry a payload of 79 passengers and baggage just over 1,000nm from 6,000ft runways. With a MTOW of 105,000lb and a MLW of 100,000lb (ie, 95 per cent), the DH121 was designed to allow short multi-sector hops to be operated without the need to refuel.

The definitive specification of the aircraft featured the original 'large' DH121 design's novel offset nose undercarriage installation, with the nose gear designed to retract sideways to allow a longer underfloor cargo hold. The main gear layout however differed in that it now had a four-wheel single-axle layout which turned through 90 degrees on retraction for stowage along the sides of the wing centre section. The legs were designed to extend slightly during retraction so that when deployed they would allow a greater track. The main undercarriage was also to be stressed in such a way that it could have a secondary function as an airbrake.

The new design featured the same basic overall shape as the larger '121 but was now more refined. A simpler flightdeck window layout was adopted with seven main panels (the two aft panels were replaced with one teardrop-shaped window), and just two eyebrow ports. The plan from the original design to have triplex hydraulic and electric systems, each driven by an engine, was carried through on to the new design.

BEA's proposed seating layout at the time of placing the launch order was 75 seats with 20 first class five-abreast (40in pitch) in the forward cabin, and 55 economy seats six-abreast (34in pitch), with some rearward facing seats. De Havilland's suggested maximum seating on the aircraft was 97 economy class seats at 36in pitch six-abreast.

The '121 was also the first airliner to be designed from the start to land automatically, enabling it to operate into airports in 'zero-zero' weather conditions. Smiths Industries had been contracted by BEA to develop the 'Autoland' equipment.

As part of the consortium effort to produce the DH121, Fairey was to undertake the design, testing, and production of the entire wing and three-channel powered flying controls, whilst Hunting was to be responsible for the outer wing and certain areas of the flap.

Shortly after the BEA contract was finalised in August 1959, some new home-grown competition for the '121 emerged in the form of the Vickers VC-11. First revealed to the world by *Flight* in August 1959, the VC-11 was effectively a scaled down VC-10 powered by four of the DH121's Rolls-Royce RB163s.

On 17 December 1959 Hawker Siddeley and de Havilland Holdings agreed to merge and so this led to yet another re-organisation of the British aircraft industry. As a result, the Airco consortium was officially dissolved in June 1960. De Havilland became a division of Hawker Siddeley and Hunting part of the 'other corporation', British Aircraft Corporation (BAC), which was created in February 1960 and also consisted of Vickers, Bristol and English Electric. Fairey, meanwhile, left aircraft manufacturing altogether.

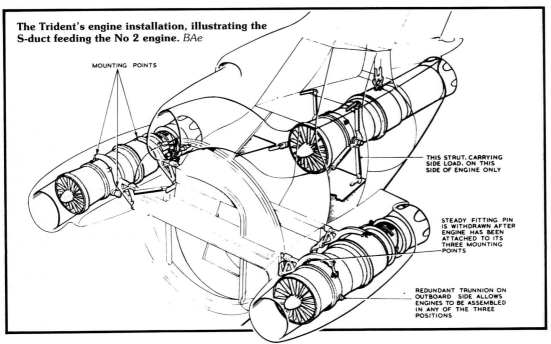

The Trident's engine installation, illustrating the S-duct feeding the No 2 engine. *BAe*

MOUNTING POINTS

THIS STRUT, CARRYING SIDE LOAD, ON THIS SIDE OF ENGINE ONLY

STEADY FITTING. PIN IS WITHDRAWN AFTER ENGINE HAS BEEN ATTACHED TO ITS THREE MOUNTING POINTS

REDUNDANT TRUNNION ON OUTBOARD SIDE ALLOWS ENGINES TO BE ASSEMBLED IN ANY OF THE THREE POSITIONS

On 2 June 1960, Hawker Siddeley announced that it intended to take over full responsibility for the '121 programme. Meanwhile, a new subsidiary of Fairey was set up to allow the company to continue in its role as a sub-contractor for the DH121's tailplane and powered flying controls.

Following the further streamlining of Britain's numerous aircraft companies into two large units to eliminate wasteful competition within the industry, on 15 February 1960, the Minister of Aviation Duncan Sandys outlined the proposal of a new aviation policy to assist financially in the development of British civil aircraft. Formally announced by Sandys on 11 July 1960, the financial support package would apply to three British aircraft, the DH121, Vickers VC-10 and Armstrong Whitworth Argosy. The decision to assist de Havilland with the launch of the DH121 was certainly contrary to the government's previous determination to have the aircraft produced by a self-sufficient organisation.

The government planned to take an interest in the risk of developing the three types in return for which it would take a share of the profits through a levy on sales. The finance would be put toward aircraft development, production tooling, and the costs of service entry. It would also be used to assist in the production of aircraft beyond that of the existing firm orders, to enable competitive delivery dates to be offered to new customers.

In February 1960 first details of a larger DH121 'Mk 2' were announced by Sir Roy Dobson of Hawker Siddeley. The development, which was 'already on the drawing board', would feature higher weights (more than the 105,000lb of the DH121 but less than the 170,000lb of the VC-11), more powerful engines and possibly reduced wing sweep.

Part of the reason for this announcement might have been to suggest that the launched '121 was experiencing unnecessary competition from the rival BAC VC-11 which although still only a paper proposal was seeing keen interest from the Viscount/Vanguard customer Trans Canada Airlines. BAC was now looking to launch its aircraft with the help of the British Government. The revelation of the proposed bigger, higher weight version of the DH121 may have been made in the hope that the government would support the '121 instead of, rather than as well as, the VC-11. In the end Vickers decided to concentrate on the VC-10 for BOAC, and the VC-11 was quietly forgotten.

In May 1960, Lord Douglas announced that a prize of £100 would be awarded to a member of the staffs of BEA or the three Airco consortium members who could come up with a name for the new aircraft that could make the DH121 as synonymous with the pure jet era as the Viscount had become amongst turboprops. The competition to find the 'most suitable and appropriate name for the DH121' saw 1,075 entries, of which 25 suggested the name 'Trident'.

And so it was that in August 1960 the DH121 was named Trident, after the name was selected by a panel of judges headed by Lord Douglas. De Havilland said that 'Trident' reflected 'a natural allusion to the new formula of this advanced aircraft with its triplex arrangement for engines, controls and systems. This constitutes a fundamental feature for reliable automatic landing.'

Something that was proposed, but never built — the forward airstair option as illustrated in a Trident brochure from 1962. *BAe*

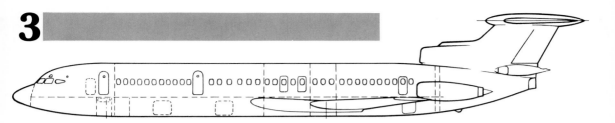

3

Early Development and Service Entry — The Trident 1C

With the wrangling over the DH121's true definition and manufacturing set-up finally overcome, and the project having been christened 'Trident', the Hatfield design team led by C.T. Wilkins was able to get on with the important task of refining the aircraft's configuration and layout so that it could meet its scheduled first delivery date of late 1963. Since its design work on the Comet, de Havilland had acquired its own low speed and transonic wind tunnels which were located at Hatfield, having previously relied upon the RAE's tunnels at Farnborough. The availability of its own wind tunnels enabled extensive tests to be carried out to define the Trident's aerodynamic qualities as best as possible prior to the first flight of the prototype.

Wind tunnel testing took some two-and-a-half years, and saw many modified versions of eight different wing configurations tested, which resulted in the drag coefficient being reduced. Tests were also carried out in the large transonic wind tunnel at the Aircraft Research Establishment at Bedford. The aircraft's high lift devices, including the leading edge hinged droop system, were tested and evaluated and it was confirmed that the design, which was simpler than slats, was apparently equal in terms of benefits. The trailing edge of the wing was equipped with double slotted flaps and inboard and outboard ailerons.

In January 1960, de Havilland unveiled the Trident's flightdeck mock-up, which was a three-crew design (three pilots in BEA's case) configured so that all three members would face forward for the first and last 10min of each flight. The uncluttered appearance of the layout, despite the amount of sophistication built into the aircraft, was immedi-ately apparent. Key features to the layout included a large pictorial map display on the centre panel flanked on the left by the weather radar and the right by the Central Warning System (CWS) and engine instruments; distinctive Y-shaped 'ram's horn' style control yokes; three large hydraulic levers emanating from the overhead panel; and the Smiths Autopilot controller on the pedestal between the two seats. As part of its all-weather capability it was planned to equip the forward panel with a 'howgozit' indicator for information on the progress of the final approach.

Smiths, meanwhile, was working on the 'Autoland' system, the development of which was progressing well. It had been decided that a triplex autopilot fit would be required for the full automatic landings that BEA was aiming to introduce into revenue service from 1970. However, it was planned that the Tridents would be delivered with a duplex fit from the start to enable the aircraft to have 'auto-flare' capability from 1964.

Production and assembly of the Trident took on a very low profile during 1960 and 1961, although in January 1960 the first pictures of a DH121 component were seen when *Flight* published a picture of the nose section undergoing pressure testing in a water tank at Hatfield. After the 11lb/sq ft test had been successfully completed, the nose section underwent some 40,000 1½hr 'flights'.

Production of the first Trident had commenced on 29 July 1959 with the construction of components, like the design, split amongst the partners. The wings and three-quarters of the fuselage including the nose were to be constructed by the de Havilland division at Hatfield, with the forward

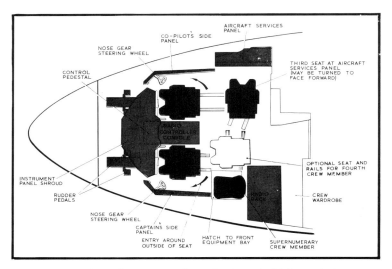

Plan view of the Trident's flightdeck layout. Note the P3 seat moves and turns to allow all three crew to face forward during the critical stages of the flight. *BAe*

fuselage (except nose) initially manufactured at the old Airspeed works at Portsmouth airport. This was later to be transferred to the Hawarden, Chester, plant, a former Shadow Factory which de Havilland had acquired in 1948 and was a final assembly line for the Comet 4 series.

Fairey was responsible for the moving parts of the tail and the powered flying controls, whilst Hunting undertook construction of the flaps on the first three aircraft. Production was geared to allow a rate of up to six aircraft per month eventually to be achieved.

The first production nose structure was completed at Hatfield by March 1960. Final assembly of the first aircraft commenced soon after when the first forward fuselage section arrived from Portsmouth on 5 April, which was readied for mating. As the first Trident took shape at Hatfield during mid-1960, it was rather apt that the last of the Comet 4Bs for BEA were being completed under

the same roof, production of which was being transferred to Chester after several years of simultaneous assembly.

As mentioned earlier, in February 1960 first details of a bigger DH121 'Mk 2' were announced by Sir Roy Dobson of Hawker Siddeley, aimed at the longer range 727 market. Whilst studies continued of the larger development, Hawker Siddeley also undertook a more simple development of the basic aircraft for its current and potential customers. A longer range version of the Trident was revealed in January 1960 which would feature an increased 112,000lb gross weight, centre section fuel and a range of 1,400 miles with full payload from a 6,700ft runway. Despite a number of false starts and projected export developments (described in detail in the next chapter), this higher weight model eventually evolved into the Trident 1C of late 1961, which was to become BEA's initial production Trident.

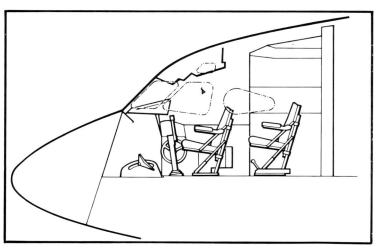

Side view of the Trident's flightdeck compartment. *BAe*

It is now known that when the Trident was designed in the late 1950s, the aircraft was tailored so tightly around BEA's need for a short range aircraft with very low operating costs that the standard of passenger amenities assumed for the aircraft was somewhat lower than those which were required when the Trident became operational (ie, no allowance was made for hot meals on board, or for reclining seats). As the design was refined and BEA required the incorporation of more cabin equipment, it was found necessary to increase the gross weight, and by the second half of 1961 de Havilland had decided to adopt 107,000lb as the MTOW for the standard aircraft. A higher weight option, the

The first Trident, G-ARPA, was rolled out in front of a small gathering at Hatfield in the late afternoon of Friday, 4 August 1961. At this time she was fitted only with non-flight rated Speys. *BAe*

Trident production at Hatfield took place in almost complete secrecy during 1960 and 1961, with very little seen of the line. This was one of the first pictures released and shows the first four Tridents under final assembly. The airframes moved down the line backwards to facilitate the fitment of the tails at the far end of the building where height clearance was less of a problem. *BAe*

Mk 1C, was available with a MTOW of 115,000lb and the centre section fuel. The 1C was in fact to be the first production model and all BEA's 24 aircraft were to be 1Cs, but without the centre fuel, and hence the 107,000lb version was dropped.

Despite the cancellation of the Medway-powered DH121 in 1958, a small batch of engines was produced in the late 1950s and Rolls-Royce projected a number of potential applications for this orphaned engine. In November 1961, the Avro division of Hawker Siddeley proposed a develop-

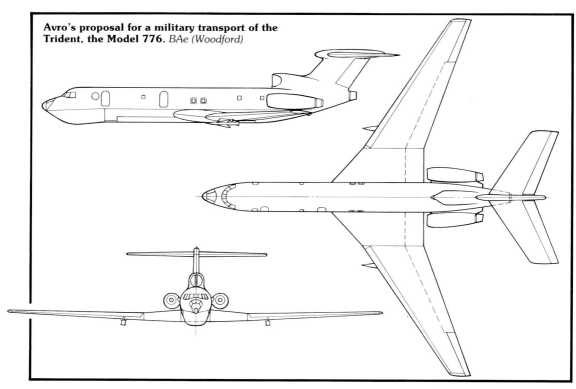

Avro's proposal for a military transport of the Trident, the Model 776. *BAe (Woodford)*

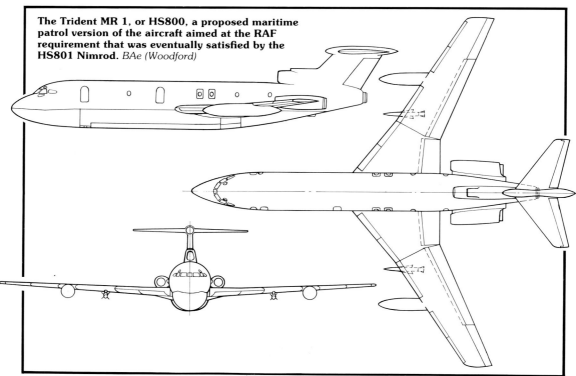

The Trident MR 1, or HS800, a proposed maritime patrol version of the aircraft aimed at the RAF requirement that was eventually satisfied by the HS801 Nimrod. *BAe (Woodford)*

ment of the Trident with an enlarged wing and more powerful engines to meet a maritime patrol/troop transport requirement for the Royal Air Force. The proposal, given the Avro project number 776, had a gross weight of 179,600lb and was powered by three 16,300lb thrust Medways. In the maritime patrol role the '776 would be able to transit to the patrol area at a speed of 460kts and would be capable of loitering for long periods of time with the centre engine shut down. A troop carrying version of the aircraft would be able to carry 103 passengers on sectors of up to 4,830nm.

A Douglas Skybolt missile stand-off launcher version of the '776 was also proposed, with one missile mounted under each wing. Indeed similar developments of both the VC-10 and Avro Vulcan were also proposed at about this time.

A more sophisticated maritime patrol requirement was issued in June 1963 for which a Spey-powered, re-winged Trident, the HS800, was proposed. This featured a pannier attached to the lower fuselage to carry weapon loads and other equipment. In the end, Hawker Siddeley's modified Comet 4 proposal, the HS801, was selected and became the Nimrod.

Very little was seen of the Trident assembly line, but the new machine was proudly unveiled to the world at 5.30pm on the warm sunny evening of Friday, 4 August 1961 when the first Trident, registered G-ARPA, manufacturer's serial number (msn) 2101, was rolled out at Hatfield. Equipped with only two Speys, and wearing the full BEA 'Red Square' colour scheme, the roll-out of Papa Alpha was witnessed by Sir Geoffrey de Havilland along with de Havilland's Chief Pilot and director John Cunningham, Managing Director H.G. Sturgeon, Chief Designer J.P. Smith, and Technical Director C.T. Wilkins.

Rather fittingly, the last of BEA's batch of 14 Comet 4Bs (G-ARJN — one of the last Hatfield-built examples) was handed over to the airline on the same day, bringing the deliveries to a close some two months ahead of the contract date.

G-ARPA was initially fitted with non flight-rated pre-production Speys, and the engine commenced flight testing on 12 October 1961 when Vulcan B1 XA902 took off from Rolls-Royce's flight test centre at Hucknall with Speys fitted in the two inboard Olympus positions. Two flight tests were carried out lasting four hours. Additional ground tests were undertaken to test the Trident's side pylon installation and, more importantly, the S-duct centre engine layout. By this stage, the engine was expected to exceed its guaranteed thrust level of 9,850lb and attain at least 10,400lb. The engine had now been selected to power the BAC One-Eleven twinjet and the Blackburn Buccaneer strike aircraft. Blackburn was to be the source for the Trident's Auxiliary Power Unit, the Artouste, which

was to be located in the lower fuselage centre section.

Engine runs were undertaken by Papa Alpha with three non-flight Speys, but by November three flight engines were installed in readiness for its first flight the following month. Papa Alpha was cleared for flight on 21 December, but the onset of Hertfordshire's worst blizzard for 50 years was to dash any hopes of flying the Trident before the new year. The flight crew had prepared for the first flight by practising procedures on a computerised experimental control rig.

After being held up by snow on the runway, Papa Alpha ventured out on 6 January for five high speed ground runs, which were followed by three more on 8 January during which she was lifted off and remained airborne for about 10secs. These checks revealed that although the gearing for the tailplane and rudder were adequate, the lateral control gearing for the ailerons and linked spoilers was on the high side.

A break in the weather at last allowed G-ARPA to take to the air from the 6,000ft Hatfield runway at precisely 12.14 on 9 January 1962. At the controls for the Trident's 1hr 21min flight was the de Havilland chief test pilot John Cunningham, accompanied by Peter Bugge (co-pilot), E. Brackstone-Brown ('Brax') (flight engineer), Anthony Fairbrother (flight test manager), John Johnston and John Marshall (flight observers).

The test flight involved a take-off at around 90,000lb gross weight, with the aircraft lifting off at around the 3,000ft mark at a speed of 130kt. Papa Alpha reached a maximum altitude of 15,000ft and achieved a maximum speed of 330kt (380 mph) at 12,000ft. During the flight, a problem with the undercarriage was experienced during a routine deployment/retraction test. The starboard mainwheel jammed semi-retracted against the undercarriage door. The problem was overcome by Brax, who had the bright idea of depressurising the relevant hydraulic systems, to allow the gear and door to freefall.

On its return, the Trident made a low pass along the runway with flaps and undercarriage down, before making a climbing turn to port and completing one last circuit to land. The thrust reversers, which were fitted to the pod engines, were used during the landing roll and Papa Alpha was brought to a halt in around 3,000ft. The aircraft taxied in and was swamped by all and sundry. In all the excitement, the engines were momentarily forgotten about and were left happily whirring away quietly at the back.

Commenting on the first flight, John Cunningham said, 'I am delighted with the Trident's handling qualities, she is superb to fly'. Three Tridents were to participate in what was planned to be a 800-1,000hr flight test programme which was due

After the fitment of flight-rated Speys in November, ground testing could begin in earnest. Here Papa Alpha is seen undergoing checks shortly before her first flight. *D. M. Stroud collection*

to be completed with the awarding of its Certificate of Airworthiness and first deliveries in June 1963.

Speaking at the first flight ceremony, Mr. H. G. Sturgeon, Managing Director of Hawker Siddeley's de Havilland division, said of the 727 and the Trident that though both were cast in the same mould they were quite different. 'Ours is of a size that will match airline needs more exactly than any other coming along in the next five years.' Lord Douglas, Chairman of BEA, said 'This is a great day for BEA. The Trident has a big edge on any comparable airliner in sight.' The fact remained that to date only one airline, BEA, had come forward and ordered the aircraft, and Sir Aubrey remarked that 'we didn't sell any Comets until the first one had flown. People don't believe in brochures any more.' He

also revealed that there had been sales enquiries to justify a second production batch of 25 aircraft.

The preliminary flight test phase of 43hr was completed on schedule on 28 February, and by the time the second Trident G-ARPB made its first flight on Sunday 20 May, Papa Alpha had completed some 118hr in 111 trouble-free flights, putting it 12hr ahead of schedule. Papa Bravo, which had a partly furnished forward cabin, was to be used mainly for system testing. Commenting on the trials to date, de Havilland stated that there had been 'a marked absence of engineering faults of any kind and there have been only three occasions on which take-off has been even slightly delayed by snags'.

The initial flight tests consisted of general handling assessments, with extreme centre of grav-

After being held up by December's wintry blizzards, the Trident at last was able to make its first flight at 12.14pm on 9 January 1962 with John Cunningham at the controls. *D. M. Stroud collection*

A close-up of the Trident's distinctive offset nose gear. On Trident 1Cs, the right nose gear door remained open after gear extension to permit access to the fuel offload bay situated in the nose gear bay. *BAe*

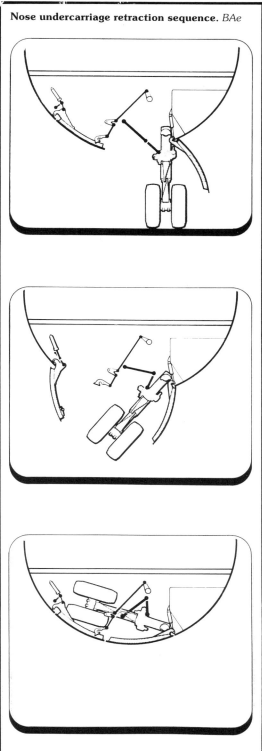

Nose undercarriage retraction sequence. *BAe*

ity (CG)positions at low speed being concentrated on. The aircraft's airfield and climb performance was checked out, as was the effect of a simulated engine failure just prior to take-off. High weight take-offs with the tail bumper dragging on the runway were also carried out, and successfully illustrated that there was no problem with a ground stall. Inflight reverse thrust trials proved that this was a safe and effective way to reduce speed, without a resulting change in trim or loss of lift. Reverse had also been successfully demonstrated in the flare.

Papa Alpha had achieved a maximum Mach number of 0.88 at 32,000ft (592mph) in level cruise. Simulator tests prior to the first flight had suggested that the outboard ailerons would not be needed, and they had been locked out from the first flight onwards. This belief was confirmed, and later build aircraft did not have the outboard ailerons incorporated. Testing had established that the Trident's low speed lift was less than expected, and it was clear that some major changes to the leading edge system would be required to improve low speed handling and performance. Tests to establish the optimum flap and droop angles were carried out and a form of movable leading edge flap at the wing root working in conjunction with the droop was tested. It was also found necessary to modify the wing to droop sealing plate to improve airflow.

As well as the conventional airbrakes and spoilers, the Trident was equipped with a novel 'Main Gear As Airbrake' switch next to the airbrake lever on the centre pedestal. This allowed the main

The Trident's chunky four-wheel single-axle main undercarriage that could be lowered independently of the nose gear as a supplementary air brake and was stressed for operation at speeds of up to 300kt. *BAe*

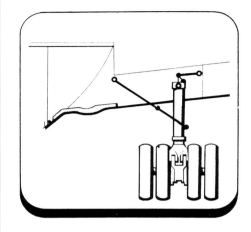

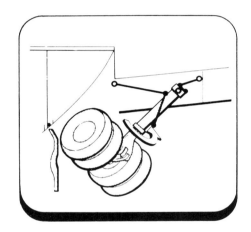

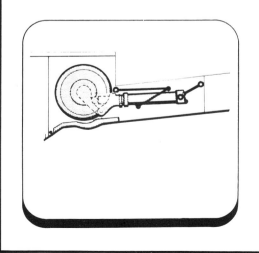

wheels to be lowered independently of the nose gear at speeds of up to 300kt to allow it to serve as a second stage airbrake. This rather over-complicated facility to slow the aircraft was however deleted fairly soon after service entry (it is rumoured someone tried to land with the nose gear retracted), but all the gear was permitted for operation at airspeeds of up to 230kt.

By the time the third Trident G-ARPC had flown on 25 August, the Mk 1C offering had been joined by an export model, the longer range Mk 1E, which had been launched into production 17 days earlier when Kuwait Airways placed orders for two plus one option. The new model featured higher weights, increased fuel and more sophisticated high lift slats replacing the 1C's droop. Papa Charlie was the first Trident not to be fitted with the outboard ailerons, saving around 100lb in weight and, like Papa Bravo, featured a partially furnished cabin. The aircraft was to be used for supplementary low speed handling tests, performance measurement with production engines and route proving.

By August 1962, the quoted thrust rating for the Trident's Rolls-Royce Spey engines had been reduced to 9,850lb, somewhat less than the expected 10,400lb. Although Rolls-Royce had only guaranteed a rating of 9,850lb, the anticipated 'brochure thrust' was some 10,400lb, and previous experience with the company had led de Havilland to believe that this would be provided for certification.

Tests of the No 2 engine's novel S-duct intake had proved that there was no problem with the lay-

During the first six weeks Papa Alpha completed some 111 trouble free flights. Here she is seen taking off on one such sortie, for some reason minus her port nose gear door. *BAe via Kevin Bowen/WTC*

out, and that generally there were no intake problems or compressor stalls even at high angles of incidence. There had been some surge problems during ground running in crosswind conditions, which were eliminated by modifying the intake lip, and the engines themselves.

One intriguing problem discovered early on was that the range of adjustment for the pilot's seat was inadequate for shortlegged crew and could result in

the wheel-brakes being inadvertently applied when large movements of the rudder pedal were called for. During some touch-and-goes being carried out by a pilot converting to the Trident, all four tyres on the starboard undercarriage burst and the aircraft then had to make a landing with four flat tyres. A modified undercarriage was also fitted to Papa Charlie to reduce the harshness that was a characteristic of the original design.

During 1962 and 1963 production was accelerated and here eight Trident 1Cs for BEA can be seen under construction at Hatfield. Notice that the airframes were apparently painted during, rather than after, assembly. *BAe*

A Hawker Siddeley engineer works on the wiring loom of a BEA Trident's flightdeck, a job that has not changed much over the years. *BAe*

Papa Charlie immediately made its public debut, being based at Farnborough for the air show week in early September. The aircraft made demonstration flights each day, and was joined by the other two Tridents who synchronised their arrival, flying over from Hatfield each day.

On 30 August, just before Farnborough week, Papa Bravo made some demonstration flights for the press. One excited reporter for *The Guardian* described it thus:

'For the first time in my life, I sat today in an aeroplane unaware of the moment when the engines were started. The aircraft was the de Havilland Trident, the quietness of which on take-off was almost disconcerting.

'...only the sight of the runway rapidly passing by the window gave an assurance that the engines were developing full take-off thrust.

'...the remarkable lack of aerodynamic and air-conditioning noises, and also the absence of clickings and whirrings from under-floor hydraulic and electrical gear, all of which is stowed aft of the pressurized hull.

'The aircraft is also rock steady, with none of the wing flexing and slight rolling motion that are characteristic of the big Boeing 707 and DC-8 jets.'

Centre right:
As part of the flight trials, Papa Alpha was used to explore the Trident's behaviour at the minimum unstick speed during which she successfully illustrated that there was no problem with a ground stall. Here G-ARPA is pictured deliberately scraping her tail along the ground. *BAe*

Bottom right:
G-ARPC became the third Trident to fly when she took to the air on 25 August 1962 and was the first Trident not to be fitted with the outboard ailerons, saving around 100lb in weight. Papa Charlie made demonstration flights each day at Farnborough the following month. *Author's collection*

After the final Farnborough flypast on 9 September flown by Peter Bugge and Pat Fillingham, Papa Bravo made the Trident's first landing at London-Heathrow airport, which was destined to be the type's home for the next 24 years. The aircraft then made its first overseas flight, to Dublin, carrying 20 delegates and their wives, including BEA Trident Flight Manager Capt Eric Poole, to an IATA meeting. A second visit to Dublin was made on 11 September.

Following its demonstrations at Farnborough, ship 1 Papa Alpha was grounded for a period to allow installation of equipment required for the flutter test programme. During her first eight months, G-ARPA had completed an average of 22.5hr a month of testing, which compared favourably with the target of 23hr.

The high speed flutter tests commenced with Papa Alpha in the autumn, whose new equipment fit included two electronically controlled linear hydraulic inertia exciters in the nose in place of the radar, and the other above the centre engine intake replacing the HF notch aerial. The tests involved the aircraft flying at the required height and speed over a course in East Anglia, which had been specifically selected as it gave good telemetry reception at Hatfield.

Papa Bravo departed for hot weather trials in Khartoum and Aden on 21 November 1962, with John Cunningham at the controls. Accompanying him was Capt W. R. Mitchell of BEA's Trident Development Flight. The first leg of the flight was a 930st. mile leg from Heathrow to Ciampino airport in Rome, which was covered in 1hr 37min, giving an average cruise speed of 575mph. The time, although not a record attempt, represented the fastest ever recorded between the two cities by an airliner, and only three minutes slower than the record set by Bill Bedford in October 1956...in a Hawker Hunter! Papa Bravo returned to the UK on 2 December after a successful 11-day test programme.

Having returned to Hatfield for the Christmas break, the roving Papa Bravo departed for Malta via Nice on the day before the first anniversary of the type's first flight, 8 January, under the command of de Havilland test pilot Jimmy Phillips. Also on board for the tests at Luqa airport, Malta, was BEA's Capt W. R. Mitchell, along with 17 observers and technicians. Based at Luqa, Papa Bravo flew an average of 5½hr each day. Meanwhile, Papa Charlie carried out slush-drag tests in the snow at Hatfield.

Whilst the Trident flight testing was going on, Boeing was quietly getting on with its own 727 programme, and gathering more orders. By the time the first 727 flew from Renton on 9 February 1963, total orders for the type stood at an impressive 131 aircraft from eight customers.

G-ARPB and G-ARPC are seen at Hatfield whilst taking a break from flight-testing. The wings of Papa Charlie were painted black for airflow testing. *BAe*

During testing several different wing configurations were air tested. Here Papa Alpha climbs away on one such test. At this point the inboard high lift devices eventually fitted were yet to be tested. *Kevin Bowen/WTC*

The fourth Trident, registered G-ARPD, joined the test programme on 17 January 1963, and was fitted with the leading edge slat system of the Trident 1E. Papa Delta was to fly a parallel 1E aerodynamic test programme for about 10 months.

Some 550hr of flight-testing had been completed by February 1963, but there was still a long way to go before route proving trials with BEA could begin. As a result of flight-testing, several minor modifications had been made to the basic Trident 1C wing which included revised positioning and reduction in the number of wing fences. As first flown, the Trident featured a large inboard fence on each wing that wrapped around the leading edge,

as well as a smaller fence on the top of each wing further outboard. The final configuration involved just one small fence about three-quarters of the way outboard on the top of each wing, which extended from the leading edge aft. The droop and flap settings were revised, and the design of the wing root Krueger flap was changed. Retractable vortex generators were installed on the outboard leading edge behind the droop which only extended when the droop was deployed.

The Trident was also found to have a problem in that it tended not to exhibit the classic nose-

G-ARPD made its first flight on 17 January 1963 and was used to test the Trident 1E's highlift leading edge slat system. After testing she was converted back to the standard 1C specification with droop. Here she is pictured in service with BEA during a take-off roll from runway 28R at Heathrow in the late 1960s. *Author's collection*

down pitch at the stall, but this was eventually rectified by fitting a stick pusher. This involved a hydraulic ram that physically pushed the control column forward at extreme angles of attack and speed in response to signals from duplicated incidence sensors on the forward fuselage. The Trident was in fact the first commercial airliner to be certificated with this device.

In early March Papa Bravo flew to Sweden to carry out some demonstrations for SAS in Stockholm. Three demonstration flights were made from Stockholm's small domestic airport, Bromma. The return journey to Hatfield of almost 1,000 miles was completed in a record 1hr 43 min.

On 23 April, BEA Chief Executive Anthony Milward hinted that the airline was about to take up its 12 Trident options, and it was thought that the airline would plump for the longer range Mk 1E, or perhaps a higher capacity development, the 1F. Negotiations over the options however ended up being as protracted as the original contract with several years passing before the deal for more Tridents was finalised.

High speed trials were completed in April 1963, and it was revealed that high speed cruise was Mach 0.88 at 25,000ft (530kt), slightly faster than expected. In testing, the Trident had achieved Mach 0.96 (652mph) in shallow dives at altitudes between 30,000 and 24,000ft. The Trident was destined to share the honour with the Convair 990 of being the fastest subsonic airliner in service.

The fifth Trident, G-ARPE, which was the first fully furnished example, made its first flight on 3 June 1963, having been delayed slightly to allow the incorporation of the first set of low speed modifications in production form. She immediately departed to Paris to display at the opening day of the Le Bourget air show before returning to continue testing. The aircraft was destined to be used for BEA acceptance checks. During the summer more hot and high trials were carried out in Cairo and Torrejon US Air Force base near Madrid.

By October 1963, BEA pilot training had commenced at Hatfield. BEA's first Trident 1C, G-ARPF, was delivered on 13 December 1963, having first flown on 18 October. Papa Fox was immediately used for crew training at Stansted during which it was flown by the Duke of Edinburgh on a 75min flight, who expressed great interest in the type. The leading edge slat-equipped Papa Delta meanwhile carried out stall tests fitted with a tail parachute installation.

G-ARPE returned to Hatfield on 29 October after completing a 35,000 mile, 80 flight-hour sales demonstration and route proving tour of the Far East. Demonstration flights had been given to airlines in five countries: Japan, Hong Kong, Singapore, Pakistan and Syria. On its return, the aircraft was put into the Hawker Siddeley Group's Avro Whitworth Division plant at Bitteswell to bring it up to the latest mod standard to allow it to commence route proving with BEA. In early December, Papa Echo carried out a series of demonstration flights for Alitalia at Rome's Fiumicino airport.

A substantial amount of Papa Echo's flying time on the sales tour was put towards the mandatory 200 hours of route proving required for the Certificate of Airworthiness (C of A). Flown jointly by de Havilland and BEA flight and cabin crews, the BEA route proving which commenced on 12 December involved flights from Heathrow to some 16 airports in 11 countries. The 16-day, 133hr BEA route proving programme was completed in early January and saw some 61,000 miles flown. Most of the flying was carried out between Heathrow and

During October 1963 G-ARPE carried out a 35,000-mile, 80 flight-hour sales demonstration and route proving tour of the Far East. Demonstration flights had been given to airlines in five countries: Japan, Hong Kong, Singapore, Pakistan and Syria. Here she is pictured at Tokyo coming under the scrutiny of JAL's engineers.
D. M. Stroud collection

The flight shed at Hatfield with six Tridents and one HS125 in the picture. *BAe*

Rome, Madrid and Athens, although other airports visited included Zurich, Lisbon, Nice, Frankfurt, Paris, Copenhagen, Stockholm, Helsinki, Prestwick and Manchester. Some 8hr 20min flying per day was averaged, with a typical day involving sectors such as London-Rome-Madrid-London-Rome-London for a total of 4,320 miles/9hr 20mins flying. On several occasions fog at Heathrow saw diversions to Paris, Madrid and Prestwick. Only a handful of minor technical problems were encountered during the period.

The final flight assessment by the Air Registration Board in preparation for the C of A took place in January 1964 at Torrejon Air Force base. Final autopilot and systems testing were carried out at Hatfield soon after, and on 18 February 1964 the Trident received its C of A after some 1,600hr of flight testing. The Trident was also the first airliner to be approved with a duplex flight control system.

G-ARPG flew on 9 January 1964 and by February 1964 the seven Tridents had completed a total of 2,300 flying hours, of which just under 1,600 had been used in direct development, with the split as follows - low and high speed handling 31 per cent, systems and engineering tests 29 per cent, performance 22 per cent, autopilot 18 per cent.

BEA planned to have three Tridents in service by 31 March. Trident 1C G-ARPG was officially delivered on 19 February and was flown to Heathrow for its naming ceremony on 28 February. At the presentation Lord Douglas said, 'While others wax lyrical about supersonic airliners, I pin my faith on the Trident. We have bought British aeroplanes not because we were instructed to do so, but because we consider them to be the best available tools for the job in hand.' BEA's planned purchase of Trident 1Fs stood at 24. Lord

Bottom right:
A view of the production line at Hatfield during 1964. *BAe*

Douglas's wife poured a bottle of champagne over Papa Golf's nose, and pronounced, 'I name this aircraft Trident. May God bless her and all who fly in her.'

On 3 March, Papa Bravo carried out the Trident's first automatic landings under the watchful eyes of Jimmy Phillips. In all, 10 automatic landings were carried out, six at RAE Bedford and four at Hatfield, all using the Smiths duplex flight control system. Five days later on 8 March, a BEA Trident set a new speed record for Stockholm to London, completing the 900 miles in 1hr 40min, eclipsing the 1hr 55min record held by a BEA Comet 4B.

The Trident's first revenue earning flight was made on 11 March by G-ARPG, on the morning flight from Heathrow to Copenhagen substituting for a Comet 4. On board for the inaugural service were 79 rather surprised passengers. Later the same day, Papa Golf operated a London-Dusseldorf

'While others wax lyrical about supersonic airliners, I pin my faith on the Trident.' So spoke Lord Douglas at the Trident's naming ceremony at Heathrow on 28 February 1964, which saw a bottle of wine poured over G-ARPG's nose. Papa Golf inaugurated Trident revenue services when it operated a London-Copenhagen service on 11 March, substituting for a Comet. *APN*

service. Up until 1 April when the Trident was to officially enter service, it continued to fly *ad hoc* on normal scheduled services mostly to Geneva and Nice at a frequency of about four per week.

As delivered, BEA's Trident 1Cs could seat 80 passengers in a mixed class layout, with four-abreast first class seating convertible to six-abreast economy. Up to 93 passengers could be accommodated in a single class six-abreast layout. The Tridents were equipped with two galleys, one forward

and one central, and three toilets, one adjacent to the forward galley and two aft. The seating layout was novel in that the forward cabin featured a couple of rows of aft-facing seats, whilst the main cabin had three aft-facing rows extending as far back as the overwing exits.

Papa Golf launched the scheduled Trident services on 1 April 1964, operating the 09.50 London-Zurich flight BE564. This route and London-Nice were operated daily from 1 April, with London-Frankfurt and Geneva added the following month.

Services to Helsinki, Stockholm, Copenhagen, Milan and Rome were added throughout the summer. By the end of the year, Tridents were also flying to Valencia, Brussels, Barcelona, Munich, Prague, Venice and Vienna.

A little piece of BEA history was made on the Thursday before Easter 1964 when BEA's outgoing Chairman Lord Douglas completed his farewell flight with the airline, flying on Trident G-ARPG on the type's inaugural service to Vienna. At the ceremony, Lord Douglas was piped aboard the Trident by a Scots Piper. The trip to Vienna took 1hr 40min. Lord Douglas was succeeded by the former Chief Executive Anthony Milward, who in turn was replaced as Chief Executive by Henry Marking.

The Trident got off to a promising start and BEA's new Chairman Anthony Milward praised the

Tridents on parade: Trident 1s G-ARPJ, 'PO and 'PI await passengers on the ramp at Heathrow during 1965. By now grey undersides had replaced the original polished metal finish. *BAe*

Trident at his first press conference. 'On the London-Frankfurt route, the hottest and most competitive on which there are 18 different jet airline flights a day, we could not hold our own with the Viscount, but with the Trident we have increased our load factor by 10 per cent since June.' Milward had also revealed that he expected the Trident to cost around £10 million to introduce, around twice that of the Vanguard.

Meanwhile the Trident's overseas competitor, the 727, suddenly loomed as large as life in Europe during May 1964, when Lufthansa began operating the type on its regional routes.

Shortly after introduction into BEA service, the Trident began suffering a mysterious spate of surg-

Top:
Hawker Siddeley displayed its test hack G-ARPB at the 1964 Farnborough Air Show. *APN*

Above:
Four BEA Trident 1s await passengers lined up in front of the Europa Terminal at Heathrow, whilst a fifth completes its pushback prior to departure. *Author's collection*

ing in the centre engine, something that had never occurred during flight-testing. De Havilland launched a test programme at Hatfield to investigate the problem and Rolls-Royce carried out tests on the engine at Derby. The cure was found to be

The view of the Tourist Class cabin on board a BEA Trident 1 looking aft. Note the rear-facing seats in the foreground. *BAe via Kevin Bowen/WTC*

This design of door hinge system was unique to the Trident 1C although later marks had upward sliding doors that made far more efficient use of the space. *BAe via Kevin Bowen/WTC*

the installation of four vortex generators in the No 2 engine intake. Putting these problems into perspective, Anthony Milward stated that 'teething problems with the Trident have so far been remarkably few, which is particularly gratifying in view of the fact that the aircraft represents such a technological advance over its predecessors'.

Rumours that the Trident 1C's performance was below par on some BEA sectors began circulating in June 1964 after the aircraft had been in service for several months. BEA conceded that on certain routes the Trident could not operate with a full load, either because of runway limitations and obstacles, or hot temperatures at the destination. Other routes could not be operated nonstop, such as London-Athens, although BEA explained that when the Trident specification was decided upon in 1959, such single stage operations were not envisaged. The problem of the higher than anticipated weight of the Trident combined with the lower than expected thrust from the Speys had seemingly caught up with the aircraft. It was revealed in 1966 that all the Trident 1Cs were to be re-engined with 5 per cent more powerful Spey 1As.

In the summer of 1964, the three test Tridents were sent to the Bitteswell plant for the removal of test equipment. Papa Charlie was the first of the

Trident 1C G-ARPU pictured on finals to Heathrow, shows off its new 'Trident' titles which were applied to the centre engine air intake. *APN*

three to leave in August, and was delivered to BEA the following month. Papa Bravo had been officially delivered to BEA in June 1964, but had been immediately leased back by Hawker Siddeley to carry out Autoland tests.

By 31 March 1965, when the Trident had completed one year in service, 14 of the type had been delivered to the airline. During these 12 months the Tridents had carried 322,351 passengers and flown 3,660,000 miles. The aircraft was proving popular with BEA's passengers and apparently the only complaints came when passengers were switched from a Trident to another type. The aircraft began regular operations to Paris - Le Bourget on 1 April 1965, inaugurating the new BEA Quicksilver Service which comprised 13 flights a day, mostly every hour. The Trident completed the scheduled 55min flight in around 40min.

The world's first 'Auto Flare' touchdown on a commercial service was made by Trident 1C G-ARPR when it arrived at Heathrow from Paris - Le Bourget carrying 10 passengers on 10 June 1965, operating Bealine 343. At the controls were Capt

The view from the P3 seat as a BEA Trident 1 approaches the runway. *Author's collection*

Below:

Trident 1C G-ARPR made the world's first 'Auto Flare' touchdown on a commercial service when it arrived at Heathrow from Paris - Le Bourget carrying 10 passengers on 10 June 1965, operating Bealine 343. Papa Romeo was the first BEA Trident to be fitted with its APU repositioned during production from the centre section to below the tail. *APN*

Eric Poole (Flight Manager Development), Capt Tom Atkins (Trident Training Captain) and Capt M. Mitchell. Each passenger was presented with a certificate to commemorate the historic achievement. Commenting on the landing, Capt Poole said 'although I was completely confident, my pulse rate was probably a little faster than normal'.

A BEA Trident was used for the first air bridge loading at London - Heathrow on 15 November 1965 when BEA introduced the novel system experimentally at the Europa terminal (now Terminal 2). The system was initially used for the airline's Trident services to Paris and allowed BEA to introduce trickle-loading. It was planned that the 'power nose loader' would be standard equipment at

Top:
In August 1968 BEA unveiled its new corporate identity which was gradually implemented fleet-wide. G-ARPL shows off its new scheme as it flares for a landing at Heathrow. *APN*

Above:
Prototype Trident G-ARPA taxies out for take-off, resplendent in the new BEA colours. *Peter J. Bish*

Heathrow's new northeast-facing terminal which was due to open in 1968 (now Terminal 1).

As part of the ongoing product improvement programme, operational experience had led Hawker Siddeley to relocate the APU from the wing

Top:
Trident 1C G-ARPZ is pictured at Paris - Orly airport, one of the type's regular haunts during the 1960s and 70s. *Author's collection*

Above:
G-ARPR greases on to runway 10L at Heathrow during the early 1970s. *Peter J. Bish*

centre section to the base of the fin. This also allowed more room for additional fuel capacity on later variants. Trident 1C G-ARPR was the first aircraft to be delivered (on 12 April 1965) with the APU relocated on the line, whilst Trident 1C G-ARPN was the first to be modified with the relocated APU.

In July 1965, BEA introduced Trident services from Manchester to Paris replacing Viscounts. By the following summer, the type was serving six European points from the airport including Copenhagen, Brussels, Amsterdam, Düsseldorf, Zurich and Paris. The airline also modified the colour scheme on its Tridents, the polished metal undersides being painted grey and later the name 'Trident' being added to each side of the centre air intake.

On 14 November 1967, the Queen had her first taste of the Trident when G-ARPX had the honour of flying her and Prince Philip to Malta. The following month BEA finally took delivery of its last Trident 1C, G-ARPB, which had been retained by the manufacturer for Autoland development work.

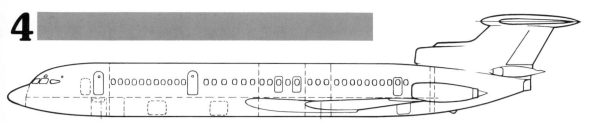

4

Export Sales - The Trident 1E

Following the dissolution of Airco in June 1960 and the adoption of the Trident under the Hawker Siddeley Aviation banner after its takeover of de Havilland, a high profile stance was taken at the 1960 Farnborough Air Show. A splendid 8ft-long model of the aircraft in full BEA colours adorned the Hawker Siddeley stand, carrying the phoney registration G-ABEA. Underneath were some 24 smaller models in the same colours to illustrate the size of the contract with the corporation.

The high profile at the Farnborough Air Show was evidence of the company's efforts to secure some additional clients to its important but rather lonely launch customer, BEA. Boeing's efforts to get its 727 project launched were intensifying and by the end of the year the aircraft was a firm programme with a healthy two-airline, 80-aircraft order book behind it. The long expected competition for the Trident had suddenly arrived.

In February 1960 first details of a bigger DH121 'Mk 2' were announced by Sir Roy Dobson of Hawker Siddeley. Aimed at the longer range 727 market, the aircraft, which was 'on the drawing board', would be a heavier, stretched version of the aircraft powered by more powerful Speys. It was also rumoured that the proposal would feature a modified wing with increased span and lift coefficient, and sweep reduced from 35 to 30 degrees. The project, which may have been allocated the type name DH124, would have had a range in excess of 2,000nm.

Whilst studies continued of the larger development, Hawker Siddeley also undertook a more simple development of the basic aircraft for both current and potential customers. Being tailored to meet BEA requirements, Hawker Siddeley realised that for export success they would have to develop a significantly improved version. A longer range version of the Trident was revealed in January 1960 which would feature an increased 112,000lb gross weight, centre section fuel and a range of 1,400 miles with full payload from a 6,700ft runway. This eventually became the initial standard production aircraft, but its development was to lead the way to more capable versions of the Trident.

The first foreign airline publicly to show interest in the Trident was the Australian domestic airline Trans Australia Airlines (TAA) which, in October 1960, was evaluating the type along with the proposed Caravelle 8. The airline was favouring a twin RB141 version of the Trident, although it was seriously looking at the Trident Mk. 1 as well. A requirement for a ventral airstair, not offered on the Trident, was also stated.

With the interest being generated, de Havilland was quick to produce performance specification booklets for various developed versions of the Trident 1. In December 1960 the Trident 1A was proposed to meet the requirements of US carriers and as such designed to meet both Federal Aviation Administration (FAA) and Air Registration Board (ARB) requirements. The aircraft featured an increased MTOW of 120,000lb, an enlarged wing of 1,550sq ft incorporating 'improved leading and trailing edge high lift devices to improve field performance'.

The increased area was achieved by fitting a new outer wing. The aircraft was to be powered by a Spey development, the 10,680lb thrust RB163-2, fitted with noise suppression devices. Significantly the Mk 1A was to be some 3ft shorter than the standard Mk 1, giving it an overall length of 111ft 9in. Maximum tourist passenger accommodation was reduced to 79, but the aircraft would be capable of operating out of runways 'of not more than 5,900ft at sea level and in ISA (International Standard Atmosphere) conditions'.

The Trident 1A was aimed primarily at American Airlines, which was yet to follow Eastern and United into ordering Boeing 727s, and apparently had a requirement for a smaller aircraft. The airline seriously considered the Trident 1A during early 1960 and it was envisaged that BEA might allow some of its early delivery positions to be transferred to American, something United or Eastern were unlikely to do with their 727 positions. Unfortunately, American was to follow the lead of its US conterparts and placed an order in August 1961 for 25 727s.

During the autumn of 1961 a less radical development of the Trident 1, the Mk 1B, was proposed which combined the basic Mk 1 fuselage and wing with the more powerful 10,680lb Spey 2s, which were offered with water injection (the -2W) to allow the thrust to be maintained at higher ambient temperatures. The aircraft also featured a higher gross weight (121,500lb) and featured a 1,000 Imp gal centre section fuel tank giving a maximum range of 2,250 miles with 104 passengers. This proposal was offered to TAA in May 1961.

In July 1961 the Dutch airline KLM was rumoured to be seriously considering the placing of

a 10-aircraft order for the Trident. The airline was evaluating the Trident along with the 727 and Caravelle and the Trident was apparently the favoured choice. First deliveries were planned for 1964. As 1961 drew to a close, de Havilland concentrated on finalising the specification of its initial Trident model, by now designated the Mk 1C, and prepared to commence the type's flight-test programme. Consequently, Trident developments seemingly took a back seat.

It was not until July 1962 that any more information on Trident developments was forthcoming. Two new Trident derivatives were revealed during an aircraft industry debate at the House of Commons, the Trident 1D and 1E which Hawker Siddeley confirmed featured uprated versions of the Spey powerplant and improved high lift devices to give better performance.

The following month, Kuwait Airways became the Trident's second customer and first export customer when it signed a contract on 8 August 1962 valued at £5.5m for two aircraft plus one additional option. The order was for the new long range version of the Trident and deliveries were to be from 1965. Shortly after the Kuwaiti order, Hawker Siddeley formally announced its two new Trident projects with details. The Trident 1D, which is believed to have been a short fuselage development for KLM, had been superseded by the Trident 1E and 1F, the former being the variant ordered by Kuwait. KLM was still interested in the Trident and was evaluating the 1E and 1F as were Ansett-ANA and

Prior to the completion of the first 'export' Trident 1E, the BEA Mk 1C G-ARPE completed a 35,000-mile sales tour of the Far East during October 1963. Here she is pictured at Tokyo's Narita airport next to a Pan Am Boeing 707.
D. M. Stroud collection

Japanese engineers from JAL and ANA pore over Papa Echo at Narita. Despite much optimism, no Trident orders were forthcoming from either airline. *D. M. Stroud collection*

The prototype Trident 1E, registered G-ASWU, takes to the air for the first time on 2 November 1964, with John Cunningham at the controls. The aircraft was finished in the colours of launch customer Kuwait Airways. *BAe*

Whisky Uniform shows off her clean lines in this pleasing air-to-air study. She was the first Trident to be painted in a scheme other than that of BEA. *BAe*

TAA. In the end, KLM put off any immediate plans to order short range jets and eventually placed an order for Douglas DC-9s in 1965.

Both the new Trident developments were to be fitted with a wing of increased span (95ft) and area (1,415sq ft) featuring new leading edge high lift devices to improve take-off performance, especially in hot and high conditions. The new configuration incorporated a slat system in place of the 1C's drooped leading edge mechanism, and the improved lift capabilities allowed weights to be increased without penalising field performance too much.

Power for the new aircraft was the Spey 163-2W engine rated at 10,680lb thrust and featuring water injection. Gross weight on both aircraft was raised to 128,000lb, whilst fuel capacity was increased to 5,440 Imp gals by utilising the 1C's centre section fuel tank, adding a 400 Imp gal fuel tank aft of the centre tank in place of the APU and making use of the larger wingspan.

The Trident 1E was to be a dimensionally identical development of the 1C capable of seating up to 115 passengers thanks to an interior reconfiguration. An additional overwing emergency exit was to be added on each side to cater for the increased capacity. The aircraft would be able to carry its maximum payload over 1,900 miles out of 6,100ft runways.

The Trident 1F featured a 110in (9ft 2in) fuselage extension increasing overall length to 123ft 8in

and passenger seating to 128. Projected range with maximum payload from a 7,500ft runway was 1,350 miles.

The interior reconfiguration involved, among other things, an alteration to the way the passenger doors opened and closed. On the 1C the doors were hinged at the side and opened inward, so that they were stowed at the side of the porch. The new design featured inward opening doors mounted on slides which allowed them to be moved upwards and stowed above the cabin. These and other interior changes allowed the cabin volume to be utilised more effectively and maximum seating to be increased by six passengers.

Another change was the repositioning of the Bristol Siddeley Artouste auxiliary power unit (APU) from the wing centre section to the base of the fin (freeing up the centre section for additional fuel). The repositioned APU was introduced on the production line from Trident 1C G-ARPR (msn 2119) and earlier aircraft had it retrofitted.

By mid-1962, Hawker Siddeley was offering customers delivery in 1964 and estimated that Trident production could reach six per month if necessary, utilising production capacity at both Hatfield and Chester. In September the same year, Aer Lingus joined the growing list of potential Trident customers when it was revealed that it was evaluating the type along with the 727, One-Eleven and Caravelle. It was planning to place an order for two or three aircraft.

On 19 November 1962, the Minister of Aviation, Julian Amery, announced that the government was to provide financial support to Rolls-Royce to assist it with the development of advanced versions of the Spey, having already contributed some £3m

On 13 April 1965 G-ASWU departed the UK for a 17-day tour of Africa, the Middle East and Pakistan. John Cunningham is seen at the controls of Whisky Uniform as she climbs out of one of the airports during the trip. *BAe*

The revised flightdeck layout of the Trident 1E, which did away with the large moving map display. This is the flightdeck of the third aircraft for Iraq (YI-AEC). *BAe*

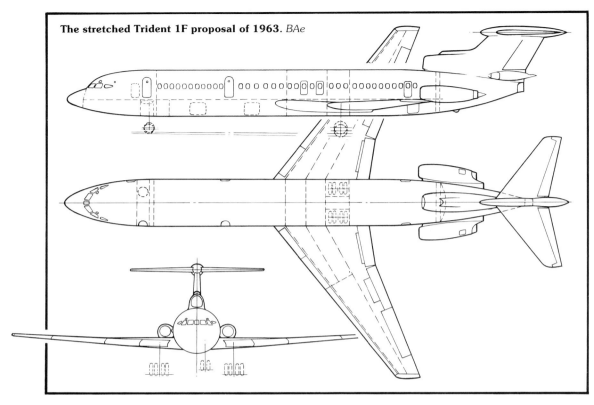

The stretched Trident 1F proposal of 1963. *BAe*

towards the basic engine. It was at about this time that Rolls-Royce began offering a more improved version of the Spey, the -25 Mk 511 rated at 11,400lb thrust. This engine was adopted for the 1E and 1F, giving the aircraft further improved performance.

In February 1963 the potential Australian orders were lost to the competition when both TAA and Ansett selected the 727 and simultaneously placed orders for two aircraft each. The following month a Trident 1 carried out some demonstration flights to SAS in Stockholm, which suggested that the airline was also evaluating the Trident.

Since January 1962, BEA had been expressing interest in acquiring improved developments of the Trident and the Corporation's intentions were made clear on 23 April 1963 when the airline's managing director Anthony Milward stated, 'there is no doubt that we will take up our option on Tridents during the next few weeks. I am sure this aircraft will be a winner for BEA, comparable with the original Viscount 701. The number of extra aircraft we shall have will be around the 12 for which we placed the option when the original contract was signed, and we will probably ask for a further option. The new aircraft will be a lengthened version accommodating from 100 to 110 tourist passengers.'

Without doubt, Milward was hinting that the Corporation was about to place a follow-on order for Trident 1Fs. This was confirmed on 6 June when Lord Douglas announced that the Corporation was beginning negotiations for the purchase of 10 more Tridents (1Fs) plus an option for a further 14.

By now, Hawker Siddeley had refined its specifications for the Mk 1E and 1F, which were now being offered with gross weights of 128,000lb and 132,000lb respectively. The 1F could carry 103 mixed class passengers and baggage plus 4,500lb of cargo over 1,086 miles, or 140 tourist class passengers over 695 miles. Hawker Siddeley was claiming that the Trident 1F would offer lower seat/mile costs on stages less than 800 miles than any other jet. The revised Trident 1F now featured a wingspan 2ft less than that of the 1E to avoid any speed restrictions on the aircraft at higher weights.

Iraqi Airways became the second export customer for the Trident on 1 October 1963 when it signed a contract for three Mk 1Es worth some £5 million including spares. The contract, which was signed in Baghdad, called for deliveries to take place in the spring of 1965 and took total orders and options for the type to 54. An Iraqi Airways spokesman said the Trident was selected after a long comparative study of all available equipment.

Six days later on 7 October, Trident 1C G-ARPE departed Hatfield for a 35,000-mile, 80 flight-hour sales demonstration and route proving tour of the Far East. The aircraft was under the command of John Cunningham who was accompanied by BEA Capts A. S. Johnson and W. R. Mitchell. De Havilland Test Pilot Peter Bugge was on board as far as Tokyo, where the Trident spent seven days. Demonstrations were given in Tokyo, Hong Kong, Singapore, Karachi and Damascus and altogether 12 pilots flew the aircraft, representing Japan Air Lines, All Nippon (ANA), Malayan Airways, Philippine Airlines, Cathay Pacific and Pakistan International.

Several large orders were in the offing, and about the same time, Boeing was demonstrating the 727 in the region, with both Japan Airlines and All Nippon having declared their intention to order jets for their domestic operations. The rivals met on the tarmac at Karachi and the two teams had a look over each other's aircraft.

During the demonstrations at Tokyo, some of ANA's Viscount pilots handled the Trident from the lefthand seat. One demonstration took the form of a simulated regular service between Tokyo and Chitose in Hokkaido, a 500-mile route on which 70-80 passengers were carried.

G-ARPE returned to Hatfield on 29 October and at the arrival ceremony, together with the other five Tridents, Air Cdre F. R. Banks, de Havilland's Chief Executive, said 'if we establish the Trident in the Far East, others will come in and the market could mean orders for 30, 40 or even 50 aircraft'.

It was confirmed that ANA was coming to Hatfield on 18 November to discuss the purchase of up to 20 Tridents and that BEA had offered two of its delivery positions to allow ANA to receive its first aircraft in April and May 1964 if an order was forthcoming.

When asked by the press why the Trident was not flown to Australia for further demonstrations, John Cunningham rather candidly replied, 'We have more pressing things to do than show the Trident to airlines who have bought the other aircraft. There's no sense in casting...what I was going to say, casting pearls before swine.'

Alitalia was another airline that was considering the acquisition of short haul jets and Papa Echo flew to Rome Fiumicino airport in December 1963 for a series of demonstration flights. Alitalia eventually ordered DC-9s and 727s.

JAL and ANA ended their deliberating in January 1964 when orders were placed for six and three 727s respectively. Although the Trident 1F had been seriously considered, JAL wanted deliveries to commence before the end of 1965, and the 1F would not have been certificated until spring 1966. Boeing could deliver 727s in October 1965. More importantly though, the Trident would have

struggled to operate out of Osaka's short 6,200ft runway with a full payload in the hot July and August months. De Havilland conceded that the short runway might have been 'one of the tipping things' in swaying the selection towards the 727. The Japanese airlines were eventually to order some 50 727s of all variants.

De Havilland was particularly disappointed to lose the Japanese orders in January 1964, but still had the potential contract with BEA pending and a decision was expected soon. Air Cdre Banks revealed that the total number of Trident sales required to break even would be 'around 100'.

Pakistan International Airlines (PIA) signed a contract on 26 January 1964 for three Trident 1Es plus two options, becoming the third export customer for the Trident. The three firmly ordered aircraft were due for delivery in the latter part of 1965. It was understood that the terms of the order called for the trade-in of the three Viscounts PIA operated, which would then be leased back from Hawker Siddeley. The airline had ordered the Tridents to supplement the Boeing 720s it operated on regional services. *Flight* suggested that the selection of the Trident over the Boeing 727 may have been helped by the negative US attitude towards PIA's Chinese affiliations, but it was also felt that these same close relations could well establish the Trident as a probable rather than just possible candidate for CAAC.

In the fickle world of aviation during the 1960s, it seemed that no sooner had de Havilland refined a Trident development, than the market wanted something else. And so it was that by mid-1964, BEA's requirement for a follow-on Trident model was concentrating more on increased range rather than increased capacity. The airline was now looking at a simple extended range derivative of the Trident 1E and so plans to develop the stretched Trident 1F were dropped, at least for the immediate future. The gross weight of the 1E meanwhile had been increased again to 132,000lb.

By now the first Trident 1E, the 14th Trident built, was fairly well on its way to being completed on the Hatfield production line. Registered G-ASWU and wearing the colours of launch customer Kuwait Airways, the first 1E completed its maiden flight at Hatfield on Monday 2 November 1964 flown by John Cunningham.

Part of the 1E aerodynamic flight testing had already been carried out by the fourth Trident 1C G-ARPD, which had been fitted with a slatted leading edge before it first flew in January 1963. Papa Delta's slats were made of wood with metal reinforcing and the slat tracks were not properly represented. The 1C test aircraft also did not feature the extended wingspan and so was not fully representative of the 1E. The slats replaced the 1C's droop leading edge high lift device, and to obtain maximum slat chord the leading edges were extended.

The 1E's trailing edge also came in for some attention with the area of the double-slotted flaps being increased by 35 per cent. The increased wingspan allowed the ailerons to be mounted some 18in further outboard and these operated in conjunction with differential spoiler movement after 15 degrees of deflection. The 1E also featured a modified wing fence which extended further forward than on the 1C, with a separate segment attached to the leading edge that moved forward with the slat when it was extended.

The improved lift characteristics of the 1E's wing could be attributed to the work of a Dr Kuchemann, who led a team of aerodynamicists at the RAE, and was someone who was to play an even more important role in the aerodynamic development of the next Trident variant, the 2E. The new wing featured changes to its planform to increase C_{LMAX} (Coefficient of Lift, maximum), which was achieved for only a very small increase in drag. During Whisky Uniform's first flight the new wing's superior lift, drag and low speed qualities were immediately apparent. Fitted with pre-production Spey Mk 511s and equipped with the centre section rather than tail-mounted APU, Whisky Uniform was initially an interim rather than definitive Mk. 1E.

One major change to the export Trident was in the flightdeck. The large pictorial map display that dominated the centre panel of the BEA 1Cs was deleted and the instruments regrouped in a more tidy layout. All three main instrument panels were mounted at a common slope of 10 degrees to improve the appearance of the layout. Some 1E customers even requested a more conventional control yoke (Boeing-style) in place of the distinctive de Havilland 'ram's horns'.

The starboard nose gear door, which remained down after gear deployment on the 1C, was sequenced to close after gear extension. This necessitated the repositioning of the refuel/offload panel from the nose gear bay (which was now no longer readily accessible) to the right main landing gear bay.

By the end of 1964, the Trident 1E had completed some 80hrs of flight testing, of which 55 had been flown in the first 30 days. Whisky Uniform was flown well beyond its maximum design speed, reaching Mach 0.975 (650mph TAS at 35,000ft) which was only some 10mph slower than the speed of sound.

In January 1965, the saga of BEA's new Trident was finally cleared up when it was confirmed that the aircraft would take the form of a cleaned-up, higher weight version of the 1E powered by higher thrust Speys to give it a further increase in range. Fairly soon it was clear that the designation 2E would be adopted for the version, and for which BEA signed a firm contract for 15 aircraft in August 1965.

From 1 April 1965, all the divisions of the Hawker Siddeley Group lost their identity and as such the de Havilland Division simply became the Hatfield branch of the company. Although attention had now turned to the new Trident for BEA, work on certificating and selling the existing Trident 1E was still carrying on in earnest.

On 8 April 1965, PIA signed a contract for a fourth Trident 1E, which in fact represented the conversion of one of the two options placed with the airline's initial order for three Trident 1Es the previous year. The aircraft was due for delivery in May 1966.

On 13 April, Trident 1E development aircraft G-ASWU departed the UK for a 17-day tour of Africa, the Middle East and Pakistan. Under the command of John Cunningham accompanied by Peter Bugge, Tony Fairbrother (Flight Test Manager), and 23 engineers and observers, Whisky Uniform flew the first 2,165-mile trip from Heathrow to overhead Cairo in a record 3 hr 35min 44secs, giving her an average speed of 602.1mph. From Cairo, the Trident flew direct to Nairobi (2,200 miles).

Whisky Uniform was based in Nairobi for nine days where she carried out over 60 filmed take-offs and landings for certification purposes. Nairobi offered a warm environment to test the new Trident's hot and high performance and the aircraft was found to have plenty in hand at the previously estimated WAT (weight/altitude/temperature) limits, despite not being fitted with the water injection Spey engines that would be standard on the production aircraft. Several accelerate-stops were also carried out at the maximum weight during which Whisky Uniform performed perfectly.

With the Nairobi tests complete, the Trident positioned to Karachi via Aden to carry out some tests for PIA in anticipation of the airline's own Trident operations that were due to commence the following year. During its stay at Karachi, more measured take-offs were made and PIA's flight operations director Capt Abdullah Baig flew the type in his home country for the first time. Whisky Uniform also found time to spend a day flying some of PIA's domestic routes and a Karachi-Lahore-Dacca-Lahore-Karachi round trip was operated within five minutes of schedule. The flight home commenced early on 30 April and the first sector from Karachi to Cairo involved a let-down over Kuwait City to make a courtesy flypast over what was soon to be Whisky Uniform's new home. The last leg of the trip was flown later the same day, from Cairo back to Hatfield.

The second 1E (G-ASWV) joined the flight test programme on 9 June 1965 and was issued with a special category C of A on 30 June. The aircraft, which like the prototype was destined for Kuwait Airways, then departed Heathrow on 6 July to continue the hot and high tests.

Below:
Iraqi Airways inaugurated Trident 1E services when it put its first aircraft into service in November 1965 on its twice-weekly service from Baghdad to London. YI-AEC is pictured completing one such service. *APN*

Bottom:
The PIA Tridents were fitted with Boeing style control wheels replacing the Trident's normal 'ram's horns'. This allowed for commonality with the 720s that it already operated. *BAe*

Iraqi Airways' first aircraft YI-AEA was formally handed over at Hatfield on 1 October to the airline's director general Maj-Gen Hamid Tawfiq. The aircraft left Hatfield two days later bound for Baghdad via Heathrow to become Iraqi Airways' first pure jet airliner. Flying training commenced on 7 October and a special Baghdad-Beirut-Baghdad service was flown on 12 October to celebrate the introduction of the aircraft.

The new Trident variant gained its C of A in November 1965, by which time a maximum gross

weight of 134,000lb had been adopted. Trident 1E revenue earning services were inaugurated by Iraqi Airways on 22 November after the initial crew training phase, flying a twice-weekly Baghdad-London service. During the Trident's introductory period with the airline, six Hawker Siddeley engineers were based at Bagdhad to assist the airline's own maintenance crews.

Iraq used its Tridents on major regional routes out of Baghdad and to Beirut, as well as on longer services to European cities including London, Moscow, Frankfurt, Vienna, Istanbul, Prague and Paris. The airline's second Trident was delivered on 5 March 1966 and the third (and last) two months later on 13 May.

Pakistan International's first Trident (AP-ATK) was delivered on 1 March 1966, somewhat later than initially planned, and the type entered scheduled service on 1 April following an intensive training programme that saw 100hr flown in the first 14 days. PIA's Tridents had been ordered to replace Viscounts and were used on regional services from Karachi, Lahore and Rawalpindi to Dacca and later to the Persian Gulf. PIA's Tridents also took over the 'Inter-wing' service from the airline's Boeing 720s, linking West and East Pakistan.

PIA's second and third 1Es were delivered in March and April and for the first three months a Trident was allocated for stand-by at Karachi. By August daily utilisation had risen from 6.4hr to 7.2hr, and the standby aircraft was then either stood down or used for pilot training. Destinations added as experience was gained with the aircraft included Bahrain, Doha, Kuwait and Dubai. During

1966, Richard Nixon (then former US Vice-President) flew from Dacca to Lahore on a PIA Trident during a visit to Pakistan.

The first Trident 1E delivery to Kuwait Airways was made on 19 March 1966 when G-ASWU was delivered as 9K-ACF, having been reworked (repositioned APU, etc) prior to delivery and making its first flight as a definitive 1E on 5 March. The aircraft was handed over the day before the official date, at a ceremony at Hatfield during which the airline's chairman Faisal Al Fulaij announced that a third Trident would be purchased, through the conversion of the option held.

Kuwait's Tridents served local destinations in the Persian Gulf and later Amman, Baghdad, Cairo, Karachi and Damascus. Unfortunately Kuwait's second aircraft, 9K-ACG (formerly G-ASWV), which had been delivered on 27 May 1966, was written off 34 days later in a non-fatal undershoot at Kuwait Airport on 30 June.

During 1966, the Emir of Kuwait, His Highness Shaikh Sabah as-Salim as-Sabah, flew on a Trident to Beirut to visit the Lebanese President Charles Helou. The airline's third Trident 1E (9K-ACH) was delivered on 21 December 1966. Commenting on the introduction of the Trident, Kuwait Airways' Managing Director Mr J. Mazouk said, 'since the inception of the Trident services on Middle East routes, the number of revenue passengers carried all over our network has increased by 19.7 per cent, and our passenger load factor increased from 44 to 53 per cent, while the passenger miles flown has increased by 21.4 per cent.'

Meanwhile PIA's fourth Trident (AP-AUG) made its first flight on 24 August 1966 and was displayed at the Farnborough Air Show the following month. Shortly after this it was decided that the aircraft would be delivered to the Pakistan Air Force and she was repainted accordingly. However, the plans were changed again and Uniform Golf was deliv-

PIA's third Trident was displayed at the 1966 Farnborough Air Show wearing the Pakistani marks AP-AUG. *APN*

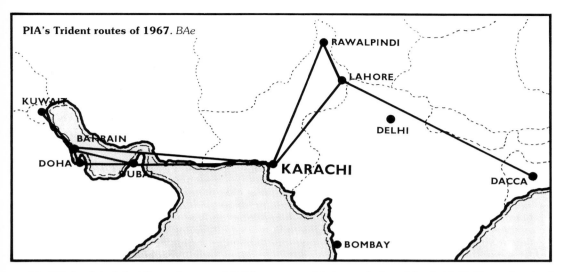

PIA's Trident routes of 1967. *BAe*

ered to PIA back in full airline colours on 13 February 1967.

During 1967, Hawker Siddeley concentrated on the development of the Trident 2E and a stretched version, the 3, for BEA. But, with five more Trident 1Es in production, it was still actively marketing that variant. During the mid-1960s, the Greek national carrier Olympic Airways seriously considered the Trident to operate on its regional services. The airline had good experience of de Havilland airliners, operating Comet 4Bs in conjunction with BEA during the 1960s, and the Trident would have offered a fine way to continue the tradition. Sadly for Hawker Siddeley, the airline eventually plumped for the Boeing 727-200, placing an order for five in January 1968.

A new development of the 1E was announced on 5 October 1967, when the Southend-based charter airline Channel Airways signed an £8m contract for five Trident 1E-140s for delivery at monthly intervals from March 1968. The airline had begun negotiating for the order only two months previously.

The 1E-140 differed in that gross weight was increased by 1,500lb to 135,580lb, Maximum Zero Fuel Weight (MZFW) by 1,000lb to 96,500lb, and passenger accommodation had been increased with up to 139 at 31in pitch. The increased capacity was achieved through the creation of a unique seven-abreast single-aisle seating layout in the forward cabin. The seven-abreast seat units were of a new design created by Flying Service and Equipment of Chesham. Range of the new variant with a full pay-

Prior to delivery to the airline, AP-AUG was repainted for the Pakistan Air Force. However, the customer changed its mind again and the aircraft was eventually repainted and delivered to the airline on 13 February 1967. *BAe*

Having operated Comet 4Bs on its regional routes, during the mid-1960s Olympic Airways seriously considered placing an order for the Trident to replace them, before finally ordering Boeing 727s in 1968. This huge 1/12th scale model, hidden away in a corner of the Mosquito Aircraft Museum, shows just how seriously Hawker Siddeley took the sales campaign. *Author*

load of passengers and baggage was 1,930 miles, which increased to 2,570 miles with 100 passengers. Channel had decided not to equip its Tridents with the Autoland equipment of the BEA aircraft.

Channel's founder and chairman, Sqn Ldr Jack Jones, was so excited about his new Tridents that at the signing ceremony in London he said to Sir Arnold Hall and Sir Harry Broadhurst of Hawker Siddeley, 'if you can't get that Trident 3 order from BEA perhaps we can get together to talk about Trident 3-140s!' Channel had apparently chosen the Trident (at a time when most airlines were going for Boeings, including BEA) because of the aircraft's increased seating capacity and the nearby support available from Hatfield.

The first Trident 1E-140 rolled out at Hatfield on 25 January 1968 in full Channel colours and regis-

Channel Airways placed an order for five Trident 1Es in October 1967 but this was later reduced to just two. The airline's second aircraft, G-AVYE, was displayed in the static park at the 1968 Farnborough Air Show. She had been delivered to Channel in June the same year. *Author's collection*

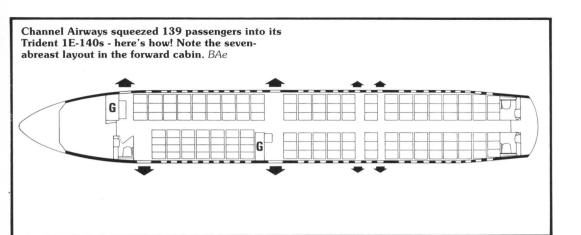

Channel Airways squeezed 139 passengers into its Trident 1E-140s - here's how! Note the seven-abreast layout in the forward cabin. *BAe*

tered G-AVYB, carrying the titles 'Trident 140' on its pod engines. The aircraft made its first flight on 13 February flown by Pat Fillingham and, following a programme of crew training, the airline took delivery of the aircraft on 31 May 1968. By this time, however, Channel was trying to renegotiate the size of its order to just two aircraft.

The airline's second 1E (G-AVYE) was delivered the following month, and Yankee Bravo operated the first Channel Trident service on 13 June, an IT flight departing Stansted at 7.00pm for Barcelona via Teesside. The aircraft arrived back at Stansted, again via Teesside, at 5.00am the next day.

The two Stansted-based 139-seat aircraft, christened 'Continental Golden Jets' by Channel, were operated on charters to the Canaries and Mediterranean resorts such as Las Palmas, Palma, Ibiza and Rimini, as well as on some scheduled services. Channel claimed its 3hr 15 min Trident Stansted-Las Palmas service was the fastest UK-Canaries timing.

Several other UK airports were served by the Channel Tridents including Bristol, Jersey and Edinburgh. In fact G-AVYE became the largest jet to operate into Bristol-Lulsgate airport when it flew into there on 16 February 1969. From May that year the airline operated IT services from Bristol to

BKS Air Transport of Newcastle took two of the three Tridents that had been destined for Channel. Wearing its colourful blue tail and red fuselage stripe scheme, G-AVYC is seen taking off from Heathrow operating a scheduled service to Newcastle. *APN*

Air Ceylon took the remaining Channel Trident 1E for its regional services from Colombo. Registered 4R-ACN, the aircraft is pictured at the 1969 Paris Air Show where it was demonstrated prior to delivery. *Author's collection*

Gerona. Yankee Echo took time out from her charter work to be displayed in the static park at Farnborough in September 1968.

About the same time that Channel signed its contract for the five 1E-140s, the Ceylonese government approved the purchase by its national airline Air Ceylon of a Trident. According to *Flight*, by October 1967 long term finance had been arranged although the initial down payment was not to be made until the end of the aircraft's first year in service. However, the failure of Hawker Siddeley to guarantee an option on a second 1E, as well as to meet the delivery requirement of August 1968, meant that by the end of 1967 the airline was evaluating other short/medium haul types again.

Fortunately the problems were resolved, and by March 1968 Air Ceylon was again in serious negotiation for a Trident 2E for service entry in June the following year. The airline finally placed an order for one Trident — a 1E in fact — on 24 May 1968, for delivery the following summer. An option was taken on a second unspecified variant of Trident (thought to have been a 2E) which had to be confirmed within six months. On placing the order, Air Ceylon had put down a five per cent deposit of the

£2.2m list price, with a further 20 per cent due to be paid before delivery.

The Air Ceylon Trident order was in fact fulfilled by one of the three unwanted Channel 1E-140s, and was handed over to the airline in Colombo on 16 July 1969, while the option was allowed to lapse. John Cunningham flew the 1E, registered 4R-ACN, out to Ceylon after it was displayed at the Paris Air Show the month before. Accompanying Mr Cunningham was Jimmy Phillips and an Air Ceylon flight crew.

Air Ceylon's was the last Trident 1E to be delivered and a total of 15 of this variant were produced, including five of the higher weight 1E-140s. Air Ceylon operated its Trident in a two-class 88-seat layout on scheduled services from Colombo to Bangkok, Karachi, Bombay, Madras and Singapore. Later the Trident was used on routes to Delhi and Kuala Lumpur.

Top right:
BKS was renamed Northeast in November 1970 and its Tridents were repainted in a striking yellow and grey colour scheme. G-AVYC is seen landing at Heathrow. *Peter J. Bish*

Bottom right:
BEA acquired Channel's two Trident 1Es in late 1971/early 1972. G-AVYE joined the main fleet but was seconded to the Channel Islands division based at Birmingham International airport. She carried the unique titles 'Trident One-E'. *Via John Wegg*

57

The two remaining undelivered Channel Tridents 1E-140s were taken up by BKS Air Transport, a member of BEA-owned British Air Services, who ordered two Tridents on 11 September 1968, redesignated 1E-110s. BKS's first Trident (G-AVYC) was positioned to the airline's base in Newcastle on 4 February 1969, where it was used for crew training until officially handed over on 9 April. The airline received its second aircraft (G-AVYD) on 5 March, which was officially delivered on 28 March. Both aircraft, which were configured to seat 126 passengers, were used during March on route proving, flying from Newcastle to Heathrow, Belfast and Dublin. Yankee Delta operated the airline's first scheduled Trident service on 1 April, from Newcastle to Heathrow.

BKS operated its two Tridents on the Newcastle-Heathrow service (up to 30 flights per week), as well as on IT services out of Newcastle to Dubrovnik, Gerona, Ibiza, Bergen, Rimini, Alicante and Palma, as well as from nearby Teesside to Palma.

In the meantime, PIA had found that its Tridents had been so effective in generating traffic that the levels on its regional routes had outgrown the Trident's capacity. The airline acquired a number of 707s to replace the Tridents and between June and November 1970, PIA sold its four 1Es to the Chinese national carrier CAAC, and the Trident became the first jet airliner to be operated by the People's Republic. This was in fact to be a blessing in disguise and eventually led to the sale of some 35 Trident 2s and 3s to the People's Republic.

On 1 November 1970, BKS changed its name to Northeast and the airline's two Trident 1E-140s were repainted in an attractive new all-over yellow, white and grey colour scheme, designed by Eccleston & Glossop Associates of London. The aircraft also carried small 'British Air Services' titles on the forward fuselage.

G-AVYC was the first aircraft to carry the new colours, and operated the first Northeast service (NS441) from Newcastle to Heathrow on 2 November 1970. As well as continuing to operate this service, the Northeast Tridents also operated scheduled services from the London airport to Bilbao, Luxembourg and Bordeaux. The IT services from Newcastle also continued.

In March 1971, Hawker Siddeley chartered Channel Airways' Trident 1E G-AVYB for a sales tour of Latin America and West Africa. Flown by Hawker Siddeley test pilots John Cunningham, Ron Clear and Des Penrose, Yankee Bravo departed Hatfield on 13 March bound for Lima in Peru via Keflavik; Halifax, Nova Scotia; and Kingston, Jamaica. The sales team was led by the company's sales director, Capt E. D. G. Lewin. This routeing was to bring the Trident as near as it would ever get to landing in the United States.

Yankee Bravo flew demonstration flights in Peru, Ecuador and Nicaragua in Latin America, which included flights from Quito airport — which is 9,200ft above mean sea level — as well as to the remote airstrips at Pucallpa and Iquitos. The aircraft then positioned to Recife in Brazil for the 2,300nm transatlantic crossing to Accra, Ghana, for its West African tour.

The African demonstrations took place in Ghana, Nigeria and Cameroon. Ghana Airways and Nigeria Airways both looked at the aircraft, and flights were carried out in Garoua, Cameroon to confirm the Trident's suitability for local operations in the region.

Yankee Bravo routed back from Kano, Nigeria via Rome to Hatfield, having operated 31 flights during the 12-day tour, and flown into airfields never before visited by a jet. Despite much confidence, unfortunately not one single order was secured from the airlines visited.

About the same time that Yankee Bravo was operating for Hawker Siddeley, Channel Airways, which was experiencing financial problems, won a contract to operate IT charters with its Tridents from West Berlin to points in North Africa and Southern Europe. The airline had initiated an ambitious expansion programme, adding some ex-BEA and Olympic Comet 4Bs.

As the purse strings tightened, Channel was forced to withdraw one of its Tridents. Hence Yankee Echo spent part of the summer of 1971 parked engineless at Stansted, providing a spares source for its sister aircraft to enable it to continue to operate the Berlin routes. Unfortunately Channel's fortunes did not improve and by the end of the year the airline was forced to sell its Tridents as it could not afford to continue to operate the type.

BEA acquired Yankee Bravo in December 1971, and Yankee Echo followed in January 1972, the former being transferred to Northeast which had been considering the lease of a couple of BEA 1Cs, whilst the latter was operated by BEA's Channel Islands Division. Channel finally went bankrupt on 1 February 1972.

G-AVYE was based at Birmingham, and operated in a 123-seat tourist class layout on the Division's Glasgow-Birmingham-Paris route as well as on some services from Birmingham to Dusseldorf. IT charters from Birmingham were also operated. Yankee Echo carried the basic BEA High Speed Jack colours and the titles 'Trident One-E' on its centre engine intake.

Meanwhile in China '256' (msn 2131), one of the ex-PIA Trident 1Es acquired by CAAC, crashed in September 1971 near the Mongolian border when it was used by Lin Piao and others to escape from the country and was forced down by Chinese Air Force fighters.

G-AVYB, the other Channel Trident 1E, was transferred to the Northeast operation at Newcastle. *Peter J. Cooper*

Kuwait sold its two remaining 1Es to BEA in 1972, although both aircraft had been repainted in the airline's latest colour scheme as 9K-ACF illustrates. *APN*

As a result of the BEA/BOAC merger in 1972, from April 1973 Northeast became part of British Airways and the Tridents had the relevant titles applied prior to being completely repainted. G-AVYD is seen on arrival at Heathrow in June 1974 — note the small Northeast titles painted on the forward fuselage.
Peter J. Cooper

Kuwait Airways sold its two remaining Tridents to BEA in January 1972, and the aircraft were extensively reworked over the next 14 months before being leased to the BEA affiliate Cyprus Airways, who had acquired two new Trident 2Es in 1969-70. During the time with BEA, the two Tridents carried British registrations and had mid-ships galley doors installed before being delivered to Cyprus as 5B-DAD and 5B-DAE.

BEA and BOAC officially merged on 1 April 1972, although visibly the full incorporation of the two airlines was to take several years, whilst below the surface it took even longer. 1 April 1973 saw the formal absorption of the British Air Services divisions (Northeast and Cambrian) into British Airways. The last Northeast service was operated by Yankee Bravo the day before on 31 March, NS458 from Newcastle to Heathrow. This Trident was to become the first jet aircraft to carry the 'British Airways' name when the titles were added to its forward lower fuselage (replacing 'British Air Services') in February 1973. After a period of carrying British Airways titles with 'Northeast' titles replacing 'British Air Services' on the forward fuselage, the three

Trident 1Es were repainted in the full British Airways scheme.

In July 1974, one of the two Cyprus Airways Trident 1Es (5B-DAE) leased from BEA (by now British Airways), was written off at Nicosia when the Turks invaded Cyprus. In fact all that remained of 5B-DAE was its tail section. The other Trident 1E and one 2E, were eventually returned to British Airways in 1977 after three years interned at Nicosia Airport.

The Iraqi and Air Ceylon Tridents were withdrawn in the late 1970s, with the former's aircraft stored in Baghdad, the latter's parked at Colombo. Air Ceylon's Trident is still used as a ground trainer by Air Lanka although the final fate of the three Iraqi 1Es is less clear. The aircraft may have been destroyed by the Allied bombing during the 1991 Gulf War, whilst some reports suggest that they had been ferried to Ercan in northern Cyprus.

At the time of writing it is believed that some Trident 1E operations may continue within China with aircraft flown by the Chinese Air Force. One of the three remaining Trident 1Es is known to have been retired and is now displayed at the Datan Shan Museum near Beijing.

Cyprus Airways acquired the two remaining Kuwait Trident 1Es which it operated on its European network alongside its two 2Es. 5B-DAE, ex-9K-ACH, is pictured on finals to Heathrow in March 1974. *Peter J. Cooper*

The remains of 5B-DAE after it was hit by rockets at Nicosia airport when the Turks invaded Cyprus on 22 July 1974. *Author's collection*

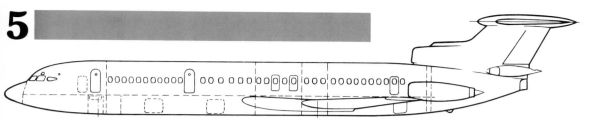

5

Longer Range -
The Trident 2E

As the first of BEA's Trident 1s approached flying status towards the end of 1961, the airline was already considering the acquisition of developed versions of the aircraft to meet the demands of future traffic growth from the mid-1960s.

By January 1962, BEA was expressing interest in acquiring improved developments of the Trident, and on 23 April 1963 the Corporation's intentions were made clear when the airline's Managing Director Anthony Milward hinted that BEA's 12 Trident 1 options were about to be confirmed as larger 1Fs, with an additional number on option. Two months later on 6 June, Lord Douglas announced that negotiations had commenced for the acquisition of a total of 24 128-seat Trident 1Fs including firm orders for 10.

BEA's negotiations with Hawker Siddeley over an order for the larger Trident 1F were in fact never to bear fruit, although it is thought that at one stage during 1963 some form of commitment was signed for 10 1Fs. By mid-1964 with the BEA 1F order no nearer, Hawker Siddeley dropped any immediate

plans to develop a stretched Trident variant, and instead concentrated on improving the longer range 1E model. BEA was still planning to have some 50 Tridents in service by 1970, and was now itself looking towards the 1E as a basis for its next requirement. In September 1964 the airline was rumoured to be close to finalising an order for 10 95-seat Trident 1Es, with options for at least 10 more.

By this time, the core of BEA's operations had moved towards Athens and the Eastern Mediterranean with the growing popularity for holidays in the region. Having tailored its original Trident specification so tightly, BEA found that the basic aircraft could not operate comfortably to these further eastern Mediterranean points. The arrival of the Trident

The first Trident 2E (msn 2140) comes together on the production line at Hatfield during early 1967. The last of the 1Es can be seen in final assembly on the left of the picture. *BAe*

1 in BEA's fleet did, however, free the Comets to operate the airline's longer sectors, whilst Trident services were concentrated in Western Europe.

The need for a Trident-based replacement for the Comet initially led BEA to specify a version capable of flying London-Athens nonstop (1,400nm) with a full payload, something the 1E could do. However, the simple purchase 'off the shelf' of Hawker Siddeley's independently developed export model, the Trident 1E, was apparently too simple, and BEA soon decided that it needed a London-Beirut and Tel Aviv (2,000nm) capable machine. This put the BEA requirement beyond the 1E's capabilities.

In early 1965, BEA was poised to finalise its order for the new Trident and was looking to introduce a 94-seater on its long range routes in 1967-68. By February 1965, the name '2E' was being applied to BEA's new long range Trident and it was suggested that the required increased range (and fuel capacity) over the 1E would be achieved by combining higher thrust engines with either increased wingspan, or the installation of wing slipper tanks similar to those on the Comet 4. The fact that the 1E could not satisfy BEA's needs, and hence necessitated the development of an all-new version, held up negotiations as Hawker Siddeley and Rolls-Royce discussed the costs and methods of paying for the all-new aircraft. At the end of July, the Ministry of Aviation agreed financial terms with the parties involved, clearing the way for the contract to be signed.

The BEA order was finally confirmed on 5 August 1965 when the two parties jointly announced the £30m order for 15 aircraft plus 10

The first Trident 2E, G-AVFA, rotates from Hatfield on its first flight. The date is 27 July 1967 and John Cunningham is at the controls. *BAe via Kevin Bowen/WTC*

Fox' Alpha in the cruise on her first flight. Notice how the titles on the No 2 intake seem to have 'slipped down' compared to later pictures. *BAe*

options for delivery from 1968. Press reports suggested that the MoA would pay around £2m towards the development costs of the new aircraft, which would be shared equally with Hawker Siddeley.

On 26 August 1965 the Trident 2E contract was formally signed at a ceremony in London. Present at the signing were Anthony Milward, Chairman of BEA, Henry Marking, Chief Executive of BEA, Sir Arnold Hall, Chairman of Hawker Siddeley Group and Air Cdre F.R. Banks, Chief Executive (Civil), Hawker Siddeley Aviation. The first Trident 2E was scheduled to fly in the summer of 1967 and the first deliveries were expected a year later.

Commenting on the order, Anthony Milward said he had bought the Trident not because it was British, but because it was best. He went on to say, 'We have made a profit in nine of the past 11 years, and if that does not prove that we buy the right aircraft I don't know what does'. In respect of the options, he added that he felt sure that more Tridents would be wanted. At the time of placing the Trident 2E order, Anthony Milward announced that the Corporation would require 36 aircraft of the airbus type with first deliveries in 1970.

As launched, the 2E featured an increased gross weight of 142,500lb compared to the 134,000lb of the 1E, and more powerful Spey Mk 512Ws which would develop 11,930lb thrust each. In an effort to meet the BEA range requirement, Rolls-Royce had examined possible higher thrust versions of the Spey which featured a new larger compressor. This, however, would have had substantially more mass air flow and would therefore have necessitated major changes to the centre engine S-duct air intake as well as completely new pod installations.

The prototype Trident 2 lands back at Hatfield after her first flight, which lasted some 3hr 30min. *BAe via Kevin Bowen/WTC*

During assembly the second Trident 2E, G-AVFB, shows off the extent to which her all-moving tailplane could travel. *BAe*

BEA received its first fully certificated Trident 2, G-AVFD, on 17 April 1968. Fox' Delta is pictured here at the traditional naming ceremony held the following day in one of the BEA hangars at Heathrow, with Lady Milward pouring a bottle of champagne over its nose. *BAe*

The launch costs for the engines alone would have been unjustifiably high from a commercial point of view, and therefore a less radical approach was adopted. Rolls-Royce found that by simply redesigning the first compressor stage of the 1E's Spey 511, take-off thrust could be increased to just under 12,000lb, and the engine did not require any significant changes to the airframe. And so the Spey 25-512 was born.

To allow the higher thrust to be utilised, increased fuel capacity was necessary. With the wing and centre section already full of fuel, the only practical area left available was the fin. This was to be sealed on the Trident 2E to allow a 350 Imp gal fuel tank to be created.

Although it featured the basic wing section of the 1E, the new Trident benefited from the continuing work of Dr Kuchemann and his team at the RAE and was fitted with special low drag 'Kuchemann' wingtips which increased the wingspan to 98ft. The new tips were to be tested on a 1E prior to the completion of the first 2E.

The fuselage also came in for some aerodynamic attention with a detailed drag improvement programme being carried out. The main areas of improvement included: a slimmer tailplane bullet; the deletion of the fin and bullet de-icing system; the fitment of drag reducing doors on the thrust reverser outlets; the suppression of the rear external fuel pipe and many of the aerials; smaller pitots and

a general tidying up of external structural joints. Additionally, the continuing weight reduction programme was to see a saving of 700lb over the previous variant.

Like the 1E, the 2E's maximum seating capacity was 115, although BEA planned to arrange its aircraft typically to seat 94. The 2E had a range of around 2,200 miles with maximum passenger payload, increasing to 2,550 miles with 90 passengers allowing BEA to easily operate a nonstop London-Beirut or Tel Aviv service even against 85 per cent headwinds.

On 22 November 1965, the Minister of Aviation, John Stonehouse, confirmed the government's support for the Trident 2E when he announced in the House of Commons that some £1,875,000 would be put towards the project.

Rather paradoxically, considering the effort Hawker Siddeley and Rolls-Royce had put into increasing the range of the 2E for BEA, at a press conference in April 1966 the Corporation's Chairman Anthony Milward denied that BEA had any plans to operate nonstop services to Beirut, conceding that Athens was as far as it planned to go in one hop.

Alterations to the Trident 2E's structure were largely confined to detailed strengthening, with slightly thicker panels on the wing and fuselage. The undercarriage was also strengthened and although the 1E's tyres were utilised, the tyre pressures were increased. The Trident 2E was to be the first Trident equipped with an Artouste APU cleared for operation in the air.

By March 1967 the first Trident 2E (G-AVFA) was nearing completion at Hatfield, and the new aircraft was rolled out on Monday, 10 July 1967 wearing BEA's full red square colours, as the first

G-AVFC was demonstrated to Malta Airlines in May 1968 before its official delivery to BEA. She can be seen wearing Maltese Cross stickers over her BEA red square. In the end no orders were forthcoming, but the airline did charter BEA Tridents for its scheduled services. *BAe*

Trident had done six years earlier. The aircraft did however carry large additional 'Trident Two' titles on the centre engine intake, to distinguish it from the short range Trident 1s in service with BEA. Foxtrot Alpha was the first Trident to leave the production line equipped with the full Triplex Smiths flight control system. One noticeable cosmetic change on the 2E was that a small window had been fitted on each side aft of the overwing emergency exits, which on the 1E was simply a blank panel.

Fox' Alpha took to the air under the command of John Cunningham on 27 July, the 18th anniversary of the first flight of the Comet. By now she was wearing smaller 'Trident Two' titles which were painted below the centre engine intake. The first flight of 3hr 30min was completed without any hitches. Deliveries to BEA were scheduled to start in spring 1968.

Some 55½hr were flown in August and up until the beginning of September Fox' Alpha was engaged in general handling tests and preliminary performance measurements. Tests included maximum weight ground-stall checks, flight stalls and

Trident 2 G-AVFE in service with BEA at Heathrow during 1968. *APN*

G-AVFI was used to unveil BEA's new corporate identity. The first Trident to be painted in the attractive 'peacock blue' colours, she is pictured at the 1968 Farnborough Air Show where she was displayed prior to delivery to BEA. *Michael Screech*

Some Trident 2 services were operated from Manchester where G-AVFK is pictured in the company of three BAC One-Elevens. *Author's collection*

fully forward/fully aft CG positions. In the first half of September the new air start capability of the APU was verified and flutter tests were carried out with a full fin tank.

By the end of September G-AVFA had completed some 46 hours of testing, and the aircraft was taken into the workshop for some minor modifications which included the fitment of production Spey Mk. 512s. The second 2E (G-AVFB) joined the flight test programme on 2 November 1967 and three days later on 5 November Fox' Alpha departed for Nairobi to carry out high altitude hot weather tests, flown by John Cunningham and Capt W. R. Mitchell of BEA, along with 30 other crew. After testing, Fox' Alpha departed Nairobi on 17 November for Port Darwin, Australia for more hot weather tests, this time at sea level. Her routeing took her via Djibouti, Bombay, Colombo in

Ceylon (Sri Lanka) and Singapore. The results of the overseas testing proved highly satisfactory.

Fox' Bravo, meanwhile, completed some 36hr of flying in the first 14 days, after which she was withdrawn to be fully furnished to allow air conditioning and cabin noise tests to be conducted. In December Fox' Alpha donned a special nose boom pitot head and carried out a number of high speed tests which included a maximum Mach of 0.97 being recorded. At the end of 1967 Fox' Bravo was used to complete the cruise performance programme. These confirmed that the 2E's range was some 5 per cent better than expected, payload on certain routes was up 4-5,000lb, guaranteed speeds were some 25mph faster in hot conditions than expected, and the required landing distance was some 1,000ft less than anticipated.

The third 2E (G-AVFC) flew on 3 January 1968 and was the first to be operated by BEA, being handed over on 15 February 1968 with a special category C of A, for crew training and route proving prior to the delivery of the first fully certificated aircraft. She was then returned to the manufacturer to

Cyprus Airways placed the first foreign order for the 2E on 26 March 1969 with a contract for two Tridents. The airline's second Trident, 5B-DAB, is pictured here pushing back from Heathrow's Terminal 1 Charlie pier in 1970. *Author's collection*

be brought up to the latest specification before being officially delivered to the airline later in the year.

G-AVFD, the fourth Trident 2E, flew on 15 March and by the time the C of A was issued on 16 April 1968, the four Trident 2Es had completed some 533hrs of testing. By this time gross weight had been increased by a further 1,000lb to 143,500lb.

Fox' Delta, which was the first fully certificated Trident 2E (called simply 'Trident Two' by BEA),

was delivered on 17 April and was officially christened at Heathrow the following day by Lady Milward. Later that day the Trident 2 entered service on an *ad hoc* basis on the London-Milan route, substituting for a Trident 1.

The Trident Twos, which were being delivered with the Smiths Triplex Autoland equipment already installed, were used on an ad hoc basis to back up Trident 1s until 1 June when regular operations began. The aircraft were operated in one of three different layouts: 85 tourist and eight first class

G-AVFO was the last BEA Trident 2E to be delivered to the airline and was handed over on 23 June 1970 bringing its fleet up to the 15 ordered in 1965. *APN*

In October 1971 Trident 2 G-AVFE had the honour of flying HM The Queen, Prince Philip and Princess Anne on a Royal visit to Turkey. Fox' Echo is seen preparing to depart from Heathrow at 0840L on 18 October bound for Ankara, following a three-week interior refit. Note the Royal Standards flying from the flightdeck windows.
M. R. Chick collection

(93); 73 tourist and 16 first (89); or 97 seats all tourist. Galley and toilet layouts were similar to those of BEA's Trident 1s.

Despite the improved performance of the new Trident, the aircraft's handling characteristics were considered to be similar enough to the Trident 1 to allow both variants to be operated by a single flight, meaning that crews would fly both the Mk 1 and the 2.

The initial routes served by BEA's 2Es included London to Madrid, Stockholm, Dublin and Milan.

As more Trident Twos were handed over, Alicante and Lisbon were added to its repertoire and it also replaced Comets on the longer haul routes such as Moscow and the eastern Mediterranean destinations (Athens, Beirut, Nicosia and Tel Aviv). As the Trident Two fleet was built up during 1968, so BEA was able to take its Comet 4Bs off these routes, and some were transferred to the airline's Berlin-based German operation.

On 3 July 1968 an accident at Heathrow saw the loss of two of BEA's Trident 1s (one of which was later repaired) when an Airspeed Ambassador crashed into them whilst they were parked on the ramp. As a result, Hawker Siddeley speeded up the deliveries of Trident 2Es G-AVFC and G-AVFG, which arrived somewhat ahead of schedule to fill the capacity gap. In the BEA Magazine, Anthony Milward praised Hawker Siddeley for its assistance in the matter, which had enabled BEA to 'continue services with the minimum of disruption for passengers'.

Fox' Echo is pictured here at Ankara on 25 October preparing to make her return flight to London, with the Queen and Prince Philip about to board. Although the plan called for a stop at Venice, bad weather at the Italian airport necessitated a stop at Zurich instead.
M. R. Chick collection

Trident 2E G-AVFI, which first flew on 6 August 1968, was the first to fly in the new BEA colour scheme. Officially unveiled on 20 August the new scheme, designed by Henrion Design Associates, consisted of a 'peacock blue' cheatline and tail with a 'high speed' half Union Jack on the tail. The BEA logo was painted in red on the forward fuselage and the old scheme's red wings were retained to keep the cost of repainting down. Fox' India showed off the new colours when she was displayed at the 1968 Farnborough Air Show the following month. In a bullish advertising campaign launched during 1969, BEA promoted its new Trident as 'Triumphant Trident Two...The Number 1 plane for Number 1 people'. Full page adverts were taken in several magazines which featured a picture of a Trident Two, describing it as 'the fastest, most advanced jetliner in Europe'.

The capabilities of the new Trident allowed it to succeed the 1E as Hawker Siddeley's export Trident. The first foreign order for the variant was received on 26 March 1969 when the BEA associate Cyprus Airways placed an order for two aircraft, the first of which was delivered as 5B-DAA on 19 September the same year. The early delivery was achieved as BEA had allowed one of its allocated airframes to be transferred to the order. Cyprus commenced Trident services on 1 November between Nicosia and London, Frankfurt, Athens, as well as on certain regional routes. The airline's second machine (5B-DAB) followed on 1 May 1970 and the aircraft were operated in 98 or 102-seat layouts on Cyprus Airways' regional services out of Nicosia to Athens, Beirut, Ankara, Istanbul, Tel Aviv, Cairo, Rhodes and Rome, as well as on longer routes to Manchester (via Brussels) and London. After a period of time in service, the airline's trijets were christened 'Trident Sun Jets'.

Commenting on the introduction of the Trident, Cyprus Airways' Chairman George Eliades said, 'the Trident has come fully up to our expectations and we are happy with our selection'.

Meanwhile the last BEA Trident 2E (G-AVFO) was delivered to the airline on 23 June 1970 bringing its fleet up to the 15 ordered in 1965. The first Trident 2E, Fox' Alpha, was in fact the second from last to be delivered to BEA when it was handed over on 23 December 1969. She had been retained by Hawker Siddeley replacing Trident 1 G-ARPB as the Autoland development aircraft. Fox' Alpha was able to demonstrate her Autoland skills to the press on 15 May 1969 when she carried out a series of automatic landings at RAE Bedford. John Cunningham occupied the right hand seat and Jim Phillips the left, and opaque screens were used to obscure the pilots' view forward to simulate the effects of fog on visibility.

On 6 April 1970 the Trident 2 was used to inaugurate BEA services from London to Bucharest,

and two months later the variant initiated services on another new BEA route, a twice-weekly service from Heathrow to Sofia via Belgrade. By the summer of 1970 the Trident 2 had completely replaced Comets on the airline's scheduled services.

In October 1971 BEA Trident 2 G-AVFE had the honour of flying the Queen, Prince Philip and Princess Anne on a Royal visit to Turkey. The five-man flight crew for the occasion included BEA Flight Operations Director Capt Charles Owens, Trident Training Capt Maurice Chick, First Officer Paul Woodburn and First Officer Pratt. Following a three-week interior refit to reconfigure her for her VIP carrying role, Fox' Echo departed Heathrow at 8.40am on 18 October bound for Ankara. After arriving at Ankara at lunchtime, she was then positioned to Izmir in the afternoon, returning to Ankara in the early evening. On 20 October Fox' Echo flew to Istanbul via Izmir, where she remained until 25 October when she made her return flight. Although the plan called for a stop at Venice, bad weather at the Italian airport necessitated a stop at Zurich instead. Fox' Echo arrived back in London at just after 02.45 local time.

Cyprus Airways' Trident operations suffered a blow on 15 March 1972 when 2E 5B-DAA was involved in an accident at Nicosia whilst being used for crew training. On final approach to the airport, the aircraft was allowed to go below the correct VASI glideslope and as a result the aircraft touched down heavily short of the runway threshold and ground looped, damaging one wing and its undercarriage. 5B-DAA was exchanged for the BEA Trident 2 G-AVFB, which became 5B-DAC with Cyprus in June 1972. 5B-DAA was ferried back to Heathrow and after repairs entered service with the airline as G-AZXM in October the same year.

As mentioned earlier, PIA sold its four 1Es to CAAC in 1970 and this was to lead to a substantial series of export orders from China for new Trident 2Es, and later 3Bs, worth an estimated £118 million. A telephone call from Peking to Hatfield on the morning of 24 August 1971 from the Hawker Siddeley marketing team lead by Mr. J.A. Johnson confirmed that CAAC had signed an initial contract for six Trident 2Es worth around £20m, for delivery 'over the next two years'. The order was the airline's first for western built short haul jets. The airline's first Trident 2E was handed over at Hatfield on 13 November 1972. The aircraft was formally delivered to the airline on 2 December 1972 carrying British marks (G-AZFT), as did all Chinese Trident deliveries, before taking up Chinese marks (240, later B-240) when it arrived in China.

The Chinese 2Es were delivered with the Trident 3B's Garrett AiResearch APU in place of the Artouste unit, and the BEA Trident Twos were retrofitted with the US-built unit during the 1970s. The Chinese Tridents were unique in that they were

Following a landing accident at Nicosia in March 1972, Cyprus Airways' first Trident, 5B-DAA, was exchanged with the BEA 2E G-AVFB, which became 5B-DAC with the airline. Here she is pictured during turnround at Helsinki, with 'Trident Sun Jet' titles on the tail. *Olli Sakari Pitkanen, via John Wegg*

CAAC was to become the Trident's largest export customer, second only to BEA, with orders placed for some 35 aircraft. All the CAAC Tridents were ferried out to China on the UK register, with this particular machine, G-AZFY, taking up the marks '250' on delivery to CAAC. *BAe*

The CAAC Tridents were unique in that they were equipped with a four-crew flightdeck. This featured a dedicated navigator's position which was fitted with, amongst other things, a second radar display, altimeter, ASI and ADF radio navigation station boxes. *BAe*

During the late 1960s and early 1970s, BEA Trident 2s became a familiar sight around the European airports. Here G-AVFG is pictured climbing away from Stockholm's Arlanda airport. *John Wegg*

equipped with a dedicated fourth flight crew member position adjacent to the systems station, in place of the coat closet. This navigator's position featured a working top, second radar display, altimeter, ASI and ADF radio navigation station boxes. Apparently the Chinese planned to use their Tridents in some fairly remote regions of the country! The pilots' 'ram's horn' yokes were also replaced with more conventional 'U'-shaped control wheels.

CAAC paid for its Tridents in cash, with a deposit paid at contract signature and the remainder when the aircraft was accepted in China. Initially Hawker Siddeley had several technical representatives based in China, but from November 1979 these were replaced by regular visits every four months. During 1972 and 1973, CAAC added a further 27 orders for the Trident 2E as well as two for longer range Super 3Bs with additional centre fuel and increased gross weight. CAAC's order placed in November 1973 for 15 2Es was to be the last order received for the Trident.

Cyprus Airways' Trident operations came to an abrupt end on the night of 22 July 1974 when its four Tridents were caught on the ground at Nicosia when the Turks invaded the island. It is understood that UN troops may have used the Cyprus Airways fleet to help block runways and all four Tridents sustained damage. One 1E was destroyed and Trident 2E 5B-DAB was declared an insurance constructive total loss as it was riddled with over 200 bullet holes.

2E 5B-DAC and the ex-Kuwait 1E 5B-DAD were both held in Nicosia until May 1977 when they were ferried back to Heathrow. The former BEA Trident 2 5B-DAC was overhauled, restored to G-AVFB, and then re-entered service with British Airways. Meanwhile 5B-DAB remains to this day substantially complete, parked at Nicosia airport.

In China, CAAC's Trident 2 fleet was expanding with the aircraft being operated on services from Beijing, Guangzhou and Shanghai on long range domestic services as well as on some international services to Hong Kong, Rangoon and Manila. Some of the Chinese cities served by the Trident included Chonqing, Kunming, Nanjing, Guilin, Xian, Zhengzhou, Nancheng, Xiamen, Fuzhou and Shenyang.

With the completion of BEA Trident 3B deliveries in April 1973, all Trident production at Hatfield was for CAAC. The last and 117th Trident to be completed (msn 2189) was rolled out at Hatfield on 23 March 1978 as G-BBWH, bringing to an end the Trident era at the Hertfordshire site that had lasted 17 years. The last Trident built made its first flight on 17 April the same year and was handed over to the airline on 17 July, taking up the marks B-271. This

was, however, not to be the last Trident delivered.

Msn 2185/G-BBWD, had flown the previous June but suffered a fire in its forward equipment bay during its second test flight from Hatfield and had to be taken back to the production line for repair. As a result, its delivery was delayed and G-BBWD became the last Trident to be handed over, departing Hatfield on 13 September 1978 for China via Istanbul and being officially delivered to CAAC as B-263. In all some 50 Trident 2Es were built of which 15 were delivered to BEA, two to Cyprus Airways and 33 to CAAC.

Over the years a number of the CAAC aircraft were transferred to the Chinese regional airlines and to the Chinese Air Force. During the late 1970s, the Chinese Tridents were subjected to the same wing modifications as the British Airways aircraft, which required wingskin reinforcements to make up for the weaknesses discovered in 1977.

In the early 1980s as the problem of noise pollution (as well as fuel burn) became of ever increasing importance, the Chinese considered the retrofit of the Trident's three 11,970lb thrust Speys with two 24,000lb thrust CFM International CFM56-2 turbofans. A US export licence was applied for in 1981 and this was granted in mid-1982. The plan involved the installation of the two CFM56 engines in place of the two podded Speys. The centre Spey would be removed and that area would be modified and strengthened. The engine pylons would also be modified. Although two engines were shipped to China for the project, it never got beyond the proposal stage.

The end of an era at Hatfield. The last Trident to leave the factory (but not the last one built), G-BBWD (msn 2185) is pictured preparing to depart Hatfield for delivery. Pictured in front of the Trident is a small gathering of Hawker Siddeley (by this stage BAe) employees with 'Mr Trident' himself, John Cunningham, 13th from the left. G-BBWD departed Hatfield on delivery to China on 13 September. *BAe*

With the withdrawal of the entire British Airways Trident fleet by the beginning of 1986, the only commercial Trident operations were being undertaken by the Chinese regional airlines, although the Zaïrean airline ACS did operate a couple of ex-British Airways Trident 3Bs for a time during the mid-1980s. By the end of the 1980s the Chinese Tridents were operating only within China, as noise regulations banned them even from Hong Kong, and the airline was taking delivery of new generation replacements such as Boeing 737-300s and McDonnell Douglas MD-80s.

In 1990 the Tridents were operating services on behalf of Air China, China Northern and China

A number of CAAC Tridents were transferred to the Air Force and took up military marks. Here 50057, ex-B-267, taxies out for take-off at Guilin. *APN*

Hong Kong was a major Trident stomping ground during the 1970s and 1980s until noise legislation banned them. B-284 clambers skyward just after take-off from the airport's runway 13, gathering her undercarriage in the Trident's true awkward-looking fashion. *John Wegg*

By the turn of the decade, even the Chinese found the Trident too noisy and costly to continue operating and the aircraft were withdrawn from civil use. Three CAAC Tridents 2Es (B-2221, -2223 and -2205) are pictured withdrawn from use at Shenyang in April 1991, minus several parts. At the time of writing, quasi-civil Trident operations continue with the Air Force 'airline' China United. *Erikki Kivikero, via John Wegg*

Eastern. The last international scheduled route operated by the Trident is thought to have been a service operated for China Northern from Beijing to the North Korean capital Pyongyang.

The last commercially operated Trident 2Es were withdrawn in November 1991 and the type's last service is thought to have been a scheduled flight from Guangzhou to Tianjin. Some Tridents will remain for teaching purposes at civil aviation training schools, whilst others have survived to be exhibited in museums. Most of the aircraft were withdrawn from use at Shenyang, Shanghai, Guangzhou and Beijing.

As of 1993, some Trident 2E passenger services continue to be operated by the Chinese Air Force's 'airline', China United, which is thought to have a ten-strong Trident fleet including two 1Es, six 2Es and two 3Bs. The aircraft are used for general transport duties and charters, as well as for some VIP work. How long this last Trident 'outpost' will exist is anybody's guess, although with so many air-frames available to raid, spares undoubtedly will not be a problem!

One definitely retired CAAC Trident (ex-B-2220) is towed minus engines, wings and tail, through the centre of Dalian in May 1991. *Erikki Kivikero, via John Wegg*

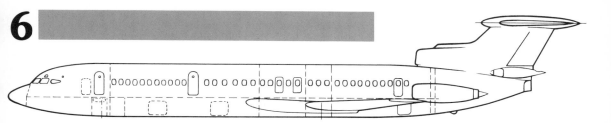

6

Higher Capacity - The Trident 3B

As the trend for bigger and bigger airliners gripped the western world during the 1960s and the concept of the short range high capacity 'air bus' evolved, Hawker Siddeley began to explore possible larger developments of the Trident to meet these requirements. The company had already dipped its toes into this market with its Trident 1F proposal of the early 1960s, but what was now needed was a bolder, more radical approach to the concept.

BEA produced a specification for its proposed 'air bus' in June 1964. It saw a requirement for a short range 150-200 seat aircraft to operate on high density routes such as London-Manchester, London-Paris and London-Amsterdam, from the early 1970s. By June 1965 Hawker Siddeley was discussing with BEA the development of a twin-engined stretched version of the Trident dubbed the 'BEA Air Bus', for introduction in 1970. Also referred to as the 'Bident', the proposal was given the Hawker Siddeley project name HS132, and was to be a 165-180 seat airliner powered by two rear-mounted 30,000lb thrust Rolls-Royce RB178 high bypass ratio turbofans replacing the three Speys. The HS132 proposal utilised the Trident wing and had a gross weight of 150,000lb. Range with maximum payload was around 800 miles.

Two months later, when BEA placed its order for 15 Trident 2Es, the airline's Chairman Anthony Milward announced that the Corporation would require 36 aircraft of the 'air bus type' with first deliveries in 1970. It was also evident that airlines were getting more conscious of the noise problem as it was stated that the new aircraft should have a noise level no greater than 90NdB. However, BEA's Chairman was quick to point out that he felt that the HS132 was too small, and that the aeroplane he had in mind should have 'at least 200 seats'. Significantly, BEA felt that the 'air bus' should be an Anglo-French project possibly with German participation and we all know where that led!

As Hawker Siddeley reached agreements with various French aerospace companies concerning the development of a European air bus, for a time there was talk that the HS132 could be adopted as the basis for the programme. Although BEA felt that the aircraft was too small, it was attracted to the design because of the commonality it would offer with its existing and future Trident fleet.

The HS132's frosty reception did not deter Hawker Siddeley and while development work continued, a less radical approach to meet BEA's requirement was adopted. This took the form of the 140-seat Trident Mk 3 of early 1966, which was effectively a simple stretch of the Trident 2E. This was considered an interim solution and would only be ordered if the government was prepared to pay for its development. The alternative was that BEA would follow its European contemporaries into ordering Boeing 727-200s (a 140-160 seat stretched development of the -100) until the arrival of the 'definitive air bus' in 1973.

As in the mid-1950s when it ordered the Caravelle, Air France orders were again seemingly to prompt a 'kneejerk' reaction from BEA. This time, it was the French airline's intention to order a number of 148-seat 727-200s for delivery from March 1968. In early March 1966, it became known publicly that BEA was considering the acquisition of 727-200s and DC-9-40s for its Internal German Services (IGS). Air France finalised its 727 order in June 1966, placing an initial order with Boeing for four aircraft.

BEA saw a desperate need for some 'interim' high capacity jets for its European network before the anticipated arrival of the 300-seat European Airbus in the mid-1970s. Writing in the *BEA Maga-*

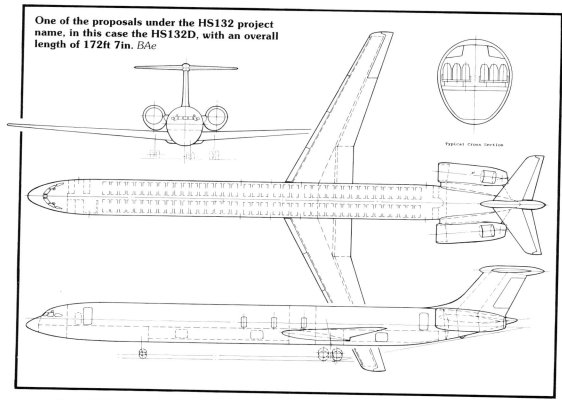

One of the proposals under the HS132 project name, in this case the HS132D, with an overall length of 172ft 7in. *BAe*

Typical Cross Section

zine in March 1966, Anthony Milward claimed that BEA had 'a positive lack of capacity from about 1968-69 onwards', and he confirmed that BEA had recently received visits from both Douglas and Boeing, saying that 'this does not necessarily mean that we are looking to America for our future aircraft needs', but warning that although 'BEA's inclination is to buy British, it does not mean we can afford to buy British if the product is not the best on the market'.

By May 1966, an order from BEA for either a stretched Trident, a stretched British Aircraft Corporation One-Eleven or even a 208-seat short haul version of the BAC VC-10 was being purported. The 727-200, 737-200 and DC-9-40 were also being examined and Milward waved the carrot at the British manufacturers and the Labour government by stating that 'if a British aircraft to do this job were available at the right price, we would be delighted'. He cautioned however that 'at the moment there are no signs that such a British aircraft is available'. It had been widely acknowledged that no British aircraft was likely to evolve without some significant financial support from the government.

With the growing popularity of the stretched 727-200 amongst Europe's major airlines, BEA's need for its new 'interim air bus' had suddenly become more urgent and deliveries were now wanted from April 1968. BEA felt that the proposed stretched 135-seat Trident 3 would be 'too small, too late and too expensive'. The HS132 was still a possible solution to BEA's anticipated capacity shortfall, but it was felt that its expected £30 million development costs would probably find little solace with the government.

Writing in the May 1966 edition of the *BEA Magazine*, Milward confirmed that the airline's plans for re-equipment would be going forward immediately to the Minister of Aviation when the BEA board had agreed to recommendations at a meeting at the end of May. He added that the newly ordered aircraft would 'not only fill the capacity gap, but will also eventually replace Comets, Vanguards and some Viscounts which were nearing the end of their useful life with BEA'.

It became known by the end of June 1966 that BEA had indeed sought government approval to acquire up to 35 727s and 737s for delivery from 1968. The suggestion that the most British of airlines had turned its back on the country's aviation industry astounded many, particularly as the original Trident's lack of sales success could be attributed to the airline's insistence that the aircraft be made smaller at a critical stage of its development.

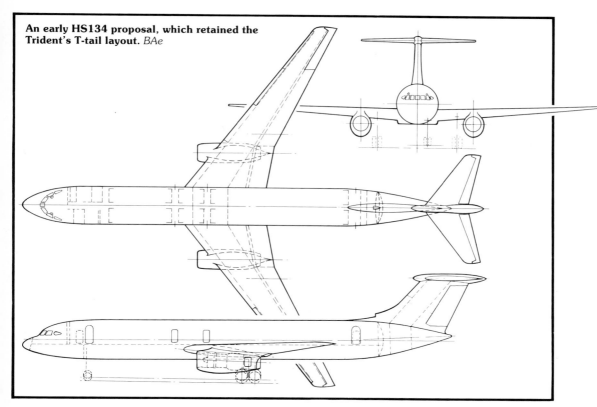

An early HS134 proposal, which retained the Trident's T-tail layout. *BAe*

During June, the Hawker Siddeley Aviation (Hatfield) shop stewards committee issued a statement urging BEA to order the enlarged Trident, saying 'the information available would indicate that the quoted figure of £10 million for developing an extended version of the Trident is an exaggeration and the final cause of strong feelings in the factory is that the original design of the Trident was for 126 seats and was tailored to its present size to accommodate BEA. This action has lost the company orders in the past and the final irony would be for the government to sanction the purchase of American aircraft because the British aircraft industry does not have the required size (of aircraft) on the shelf.'

On 2 August the Minster of Aviation, Fred Mulley, announced that BEA should 'buy British' despite BEA's selection 'on purely commercial grounds of American aircraft'. The Labour government, however, informed BEA that 'it would take steps to ensure BEA is able to operate as a fully commercial undertaking with the fleet it acquires', effectively meaning that an operating subsidy (or compensation) would be provided to the airline to cover the costs incurred of not having the aircraft which and when it wanted. It was also confirmed that the government would provide launching aid for the types selected.

As work on the HS132 progressed, a further more radical Trident-based twin-engined derivative was proposed, the HS134 Airbus of December 1966. This featured a fuselage stretch of around 30ft increasing overall length to 146ft 3in and seating for up to 210 passengers. Although utilising the Trident's nose, fuselage and an extended 'supercritical' wing, it had a completely new configuration with a low-set tailplane, new tail fin, and the RB178s mounted under the wing. Gone was the Trident's unique offset nose wheel and swivelling double main bogeys; in their place were a conventional forward retracting nose unit and four-wheel truck main gear. The aircraft bore more than a passing resemblance to the Boeing 757, which itself evolved from the trijet 727, albeit some 10 years after the HS134.

Both these Trident-based twinjets would have offered seat-mile costs some 25-30 per cent below types then currently in service and, being of derivative design, it was estimated that they would have had launch costs around half that of an all-new design. In the end, the RB178 was not continued (although it did spawn the RB211), and the required European partner for these complex Trident developments was not secured. Hawker Siddeley's offering was therefore to remain as the stretched Trident 3 and this would only be sanctioned if it had relatively low launch costs, which were no more than a third of the estimated cost of the HS132 or 134.

BEA's IGS requirement was fulfilled by an order for up to 24 99-seat BAC One-Eleven 500s announced in January 1967. By this stage, the high capacity BAC VC-10 project had been discarded by BEA and the airline was favouring Hawker Siddeley's Rolls-Royce Spey 512-powered Trident 3 proposal.

The need to operate the new aircraft on both short high density routes as well as on longer holiday routes to the Mediterranean resorts meant that a high standard of take-off performance was needed. The problems of developing significantly higher thrust versions of the Spey and the modifying of the Trident airframe to accommodate such thrust increases has been discussed in the previous chapter. To keep development costs down, Hawker Siddeley came up with a novel solution to the problem of the stretched Trident's required increased thrust, and in late 1966 was proposing a Mk 3B version of the aircraft which featured an additional 6,000lb thrust Rolls-Royce RB162 booster turbojet to improve take-off and climb performance. The RB162 was a lightweight lift engine that had been under development for the experimental vertical take-off/landing Dornier 31 aircraft, and was to be fitted above the centre engine installed in the position currently occupied by the APU. As an alternative to the RB162, the Bristol Siddeley Orpheus was being considered which, although being slightly heavier, was a production engine that could be developed for the Trident far more cheaply.

BAC however was keen to 'clean up' with the BEA order and meet the airline's larger capacity requirement as well and, from the ashes of the dead short haul VC-10, the 170-190 seat BAC Two-Eleven was born. Initially powered by two of the VC-10's Rolls-Royce Conways, the aircraft evolved during early 1967 powered by two of the new 30,000lb thrust high by-pass ratio Rolls-Royce RB211 turbofans. BEA seriously considered the proposal and in early 1967 Milward sought government permission to order 30 Two-Elevens plus 10 options worth some £110 million, for service entry in 1972. Government support would be needed to assist in raising the estimated £60 million development costs for the launch of the new aircraft.

By April 1967 BEA was again looking to the Boeing 727, frustrated by the government's vacillation over the launching of an all-new aircraft in the form of the Two-Eleven, to meet the BEA requirement. 'Every week that goes by,' said Milward, 'drives us nearer and nearer to buying the Boeing 727'.

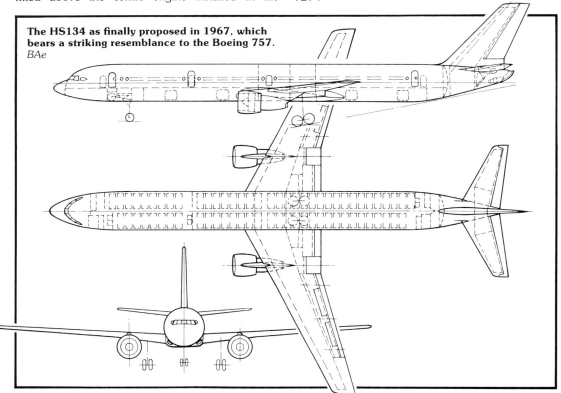

The HS134 as finally proposed in 1967, which bears a striking resemblance to the Boeing 757.
BAe

In the end, the Two-Eleven was not launched and the government agreed to support the development of the derivative Trident 3B (BEA's third choice after the 727 and Two-Eleven) to the tune of £15 million. Before it died, the Two-Eleven did however manage to drag the saga of BEA's jet order out by another 12 months or so. By December 1967, the Trident 3B project was fairly well defined with the 5,230lb thrust Rolls-Royce RB162 now selected for the aircraft and the final negotiations with BEA over the order were under way.

The question of government compensation for BEA's forced selection of the smaller British alternative held up the final signing of the Trident 3 order even longer. The plan had been that the amount of money due to the airline would be based on the difference in seat-mile costs between BEA's choice, the 727-200, and the Trident 3B. BEA's order for 26 Trident 3Bs plus 10 options valued at £83 million, was at last announced by the President of the Board of Trade, Mr Anthony Crossland, in the House of Commons on 13 March 1968. Deliveries were scheduled to commence in spring 1971, conditional on a formal contract being signed in the near future.

Anthony Crossland announced in the House of Commons on 10 July 1968 the terms of BEA's compensation for not being allowed to operate the aircraft (727s) it had wanted. This was what had been labelled the 'Mulley Pledge', when the government blocked the airline's order for 727s in August 1966 but vowed that it would ensure BEA was able to operate as 'a fully commercial undertaking'.

The agreement involved the transfer of some £25 million of the airline's current borrowings into a special account on which no interest would be paid. This could then be transferred as necessary into BEA's profit and loss account. There was also a possibility of 'a further sum of £12.5 million for consideration later should that be needed'. The plan was that 'in 1972 the Board of Trade would consult BEA on the basis of experience up to then and of the latest forecasts to determine whether BEA still needed this further sum to be transferred from 1 April 1972 to 31 March 1975'.

Sir Anthony Milward described the government's settlement as 'fair - but not generous'. The £80 million Trident 3B contract was formally signed in London on Friday, 16 August by Sir Anthony Milward and Mr J. T. Lidbury, Managing Director of Hawker Siddeley Aviation. Part of the contract stipulated the fitting of Smiths Autoland equipment at the Triplex level.

As launched, the Trident 3B featured a fuselage extension of 16ft 5in over previous models, with an 8ft 5in stretch forward of the wing and 8ft aft increasing the overall length to 131ft 2in. The extension forward of the wing featured a 20in plug

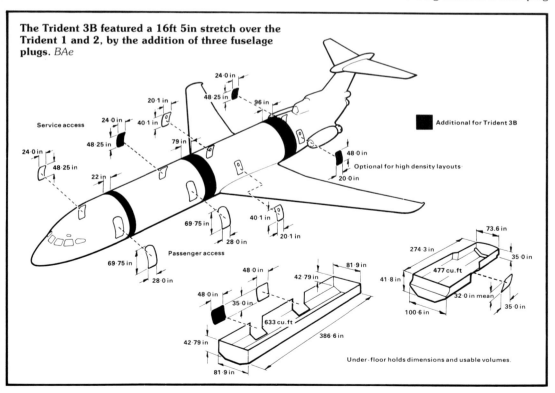

The Trident 3B featured a 16ft 5in stretch over the Trident 1 and 2, by the addition of three fuselage plugs. *BAe*

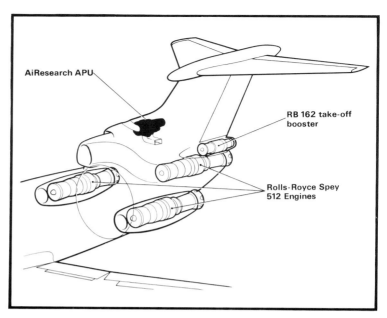

The Trident 3B's five-engine installation. *BAe*

AiResearch APU

RB 162 take-off booster

Rolls-Royce Spey 512 Engines

between the forward and centre doors to allow an extra row of seats to be fitted in the forward cabin. The remainder of the forward extension was a 6ft 9in plug in front of the wing. Some 146 passengers could be accommodated in a standard economy class layout, although maximum seating could be increased to 180 if more dense layouts were adopted. The Trident 1E/2E's two Type IV over-wing emergency exits (36in x 20in) on each side were replaced by a single Type III (41in x 20in) item, whilst an additional 48in x 24in service door/emergency exit was added on the starboard side just forward of the engine.

Although the wingspan of the 3B was unchanged from the 2E, to help lift the higher weights of the larger aircraft the outer wing featured an increase in chord, which in turn increased wing area by 32sq ft. This also provided larger span out-board flaps, which gave an increase in area of some 26 per cent, and the lift dumper area was also increased by 35 per cent. The ailerons were reduced in size and moved outboard as more reliance was put on the use of spoilers for roll con-trol, necessitating their maximum differential angle to be increased from 10 to 20 degrees. The wing's angle of incidence was increased by 2.5 degrees to allow for the same rotation angle on take-off with the lengthened rear fuselage.

The 5,230lb thrust Rolls-Royce RB162-86 booster was installed at the base of the fin replacing the APU which was relocated to above the central air intake. As a result the Trident 3B's rudder was somewhat smaller than on previous models. The booster which, when needed, would be used for take-off and initial climb, allowed either a 14,500lb

increase in payload or a 1,800ft reduction in take-off run. The 3B's Speys were the 11,960lb thrust Mk 512s of the 2E, but the Trident's original Bristol Siddeley Artouste APU was replaced by a Garrett AiResearch GTCP85C model.

Fuel capacity was less than that of the 1E and 2E, with the deletion of the aft centre tank (400 Imp gal) and the fin tank (350 Imp gal) reducing overall capacity to 5,620 Imp gal. Gross weight was increased to 150-155,000lb, and range with 146 passengers and baggage was around 1,230 miles, increasing to 1,700 miles with 92 passengers and baggage. Cruise speed would be Mach 0.84 at 25,000ft, equivalent to 581mph.

Once the compensation details had been sorted out, the 'intent to purchase' letter was received by Hawker Siddeley in July 1968 and the assembly of the Trident 3B's major sub-assemblies commenced. The first centre section and stub wing had been moved from its jig at Hatfield by the middle of February 1969 and the following month the first front fuselage section arrived after completing its 200-mile journey on the back of a lorry from the Hawker Siddeley plant at Brough in Yorkshire. The outer wings for the new Trident were produced at the Hawker Siddeley factory at Hamble, whilst other sub-assemblies came from plants at Chester and Manchester. Rear fuselage assemblies were produced at Hatfield.

Trident 3B production was integrated with that of the 2E. By this time, the last of the 2Es were being built for BEA, whilst aircraft were also being assembled for Cyprus Airways. The main Trident jigs could be quickly adjusted to either 2E or 3B to

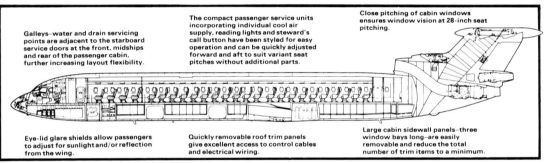

Galleys—water and drain servicing points are adjacent to the starboard service doors at the front, midships and rear of the passenger cabin, further increasing layout flexibility.

The compact passenger service units incorporating individual cool air supply, reading lights and steward's call button have been styled for easy operation and can be quickly adjusted forward and aft to suit variant seat pitches without additional parts.

Close pitching of cabin windows ensures window vision at 28-inch seat pitching.

Eye-lid glare shields allow passengers to adjust for sunlight and/or reflection from the wing.

Quickly removable roof trim panels give excellent access to control cables and electrical wiring.

Large cabin sidewall panels—three window bays long—are easily removable and reduce the total number of trim items to a minimum.

allow both types to be readily interspersed on the line to suit demand.

The first Trident 3B, registered G-AWYZ, was rolled out at Hatfield on 17 November 1969, wearing the BEA 'High Speed Jack' colours, with the titles 'Trident Three' on the centre engine air intake. Prior to making her first flight, Yankee Zulu was supported by special cradles to allow resonance tests to be carried out. Yankee Zulu made her first flight at 12.15 on 11 December, piloted by John Cunningham. A mock-up of the RB162 was installed and Yankee Zulu was airborne for 2hr 50min. Five Trident 3Bs were to be used in the flight-test programme which was planned to include at least 500hr of flying and the first flight-rated RB162 was expected to become available in the early summer.

The second Trident 3B (G-AWZA) was rolled out on 17 February 1970 and joined the flight-test programme on 9 March, by which time the first machine had completed over 80hr of testing. Tests undertaken included a general assessment of per-

Top:
Trident 3B ship one, msn 2301, comes together at Hatfield in mid-1969. *BAe*

Above:
A cutaway of the Trident 3B.

formance of the new features and the clearance of C of G position, weight and design speed boundaries. A number of Autolands were also carried out.

By April 1970 the final clearance testing of the boost engine installation had been completed to allow flight-tests to commence with the first operational unit. This was installed into Yankee Zulu which then initiated performance measurements of the engine, as well as continuing to carry out Autoland trials. The boost engine's air intakes were sealed by pneumatically operated doors that lay flush when in the closed position.

Zulu Alpha meanwhile was being used to investigate low speed handling and stall characteristics. The Trident 3B differed from the previous models

Yankee Zulu climbs away on its first flight on 11 December 1969, which lasted 2hr 50min. Early flights such as this were made with a mock-up of the RB162 booster installed, rather than the real thing. *BAe*

in that it was equipped with a triplex, rather than duplex, Angle of Attack stick pusher installation.

During June, Yankee Zulu dropped out of the test programme for a flying visit to Nicosia to carry out a publicity exercise for BEA. The aircraft was extensively photographed and filmed both in the air and on the ground, before returning to Hatfield nonstop on 23 June.

On 13 August Yankee Zulu departed for Madrid to commence tropical trials, as its forebear Papa Bravo had done seven years earlier. Take-off performance was measured at weights of 153,000lb (68,000kg), both with and without the boost engine, and at all four of the take-off flap settings. Engine failures were also simulated. After the completion of the Madrid tests, Yankee Zulu positioned to Dubai, via Athens and Baghdad, to carry out high temperature climb performance tests. The efficiency of the cabin air conditioning system was also tested. The trials were completed in early September and Yankee Zulu positioned back to Hatfield, again via Baghdad and Athens. Meanwhile the third 3B, G-AWZB, had flown on 18 August 1970 and was then demonstrated at the 1970 Farnborough Air Show the following month.

By the end of 1970 the flight test programme was progressing so well that a Trident 3B was able to be handed over to the airline for crew training and route proving. At the ceremony at Hatfield on 7 December, attended by Sir Anthony and Lady Milward, Henry Marking, and Air Chief Marshal Sir Harry Broadhurst (Deputy MD of Hawker Siddeley Aviation), the airline's first Trident 3, G-AWZA, was officially named when Lady Milward carried out the

The boost engine installed just above the No 2 engine was a fairly substantial piece of equipment, as this photograph illustrates. *Author*

traditional pouring of champagne over the nose routine as BEA took delivery of the aircraft. At the ceremony, Sir Anthony Milward spoke of the 'great five engine Trident' (ie, three Speys, one RB162 and one APU), and continued 'I am particularly proud to see the introduction and arrival of this very splendid aircraft which has improved in looks as it has grown in size'.

Zulu Alpha was used for pilot training at Stansted prior to being returned to the manufacturer to be brought up to production specification and redelivered to the airline on 11 May 1971. Unfortunately on 19 January 1971 G-AWZA was involved in an accident with a Comet 4 at Bedford (Thurleigh) whilst being used for crew training. The Trident 3 was making an approach to the runway,

The first two Trident 3Bs, G-AWYZ and G-AWZA (nearest the camera), take time off from flight-testing at Hatfield during 1970. The first 'live' boost flight-tests were undertaken by Yankee Zulu in spring of that year. *BAe*

on which an RAF Comet was waiting to take off, with the intention of executing a go-around at 100ft (R). However, for some reason Zulu Alpha descended below 100ft and whilst overshooting struck the fin of the Comet with the underside of its port wing and flaps. The Comet seemed to come off worse, losing most of its tail fin.

The Trident 3B received its C of A on 8 February 1971, after a 14-month, 700-hr flight-test programme. The first fully certificated Trident 3B, G-AWZC, was delivered to the airline on 18 February and the airline received its second aircraft (G-AWZB) six days later on 24 February. The final results of the flight-testing had revealed that the Trident 3B had bettered its performance guarantees by a handsome margin. The weight of the aircraft was around 3,000lb below estimates and drag was lower than expected, resulting in 3-4 per cent less fuel burn in the cruise. From performance-limited airfields the mission payloads were bettered by between 4,000lb and 9,000lb.

BEA's first Trident 3 revenue service took place on Monday, 1 March 1971, when G-AWZB operated a service between Heathrow and Paris - Orly

Zulu Bravo prepares to be 'kissed on' after completing a display at Farnborough. This picture illustrates the Trident large double slotted flaps, which were some 26 per cent larger in area compared to previous marks. *Author's collection*

The flightdeck of Zulu Bravo. Very little had changed up front in the 10 years since the first Trident 1s had come into service. *BAe*

Below:

The 'great five-engine Trident', as Sir Anthony Milward described the Mk 3B when BEA's first Trident 3, G-AWZA, was officially named at the handing-over ceremony. Zulu Alpha was officially delivered to BEA on 11 May 1971 and is seen here at Paris - Orly during turnround. *APN*

whilst regular operations began on 1 April on routes from London to Paris and Lisbon. On this date BEA was divided into various new divisions, with the Heathrow-based Trident fleet falling under the 'BEA Mainline' banner. Interestingly, unlike the Trident 2, BEA set up a new Flight for the operation of the Trident Three, meaning that Trident pilots converting to the 3B would no longer fly the 1 or 2. Initial Trident 3 operations were operated with the boost engine inactive.

BEA configured its new Trident 3s with a two-class cabin that included 119 economy class seats six-abreast, and 14 convertible first class seats four-abreast (36in pitch). The aircraft were operated in either a two-class 133-seat layout or 140-seat all-tourist layout. The Trident 3s were equipped with burgundy seats featuring beige base cushions, pigskin armrests, and cork patterned pull-down tables.

Two galleys were installed in BEA's Trident 3s, one at the front of the aircraft and the other in the centre, whilst the toilet layout was similar to the previous Tridents, with one forward and two aft. Interestingly, BEA's Trident 3s established a new concept for the airline's cabin service, with the introduction of a trolley serving system.

Other routes operated by the type during the first few months included Dublin, Palma, Glasgow, Oslo, Milan, Amsterdam and Madrid. Brussels and Rome were added later replacing Trident Ones and

Left:
G-AWZJ shows off the Trident's clean lines as she comes into land at Heathrow during the early 1970s. *Peter J. Bish*

Twos. By November 1971 Pisa, Zurich, Nice, Geneva, Copenhagen, Naples, and Malta had been added to the Trident 3's destinations from London, whilst some Birmingham-Malta services were also flown with the aircraft.

A Trident Three brochure published by BEA during 1971 featuring a number of the photographs taken on Yankee Zulu's visit to Cyprus, described the new Trident as 'the most beautiful, most advanced jetliner flying in Europe'. Rather hypocritically, the text boasted that BEA had 'once again decided to buy British'. The airline, apparently, really had decided to lump it *and* like it!

The first Trident 3B (G-AWYZ) was retained by Hawker Siddeley to continue Autoland trials and was eventually delivered to BEA on 23 March 1972. BEA's last Trident 3 (G-AWZZ) was handed over to the airline on 19 April 1973, being the 64th and last Trident to be delivered new to BEA.

In October 1972 the Trident 3 had the opportunity to emulate its sister aircraft as a Royal transport, when G-AWZV flew the Queen, Prince Philip and Princess Anne on a state visit to Yugoslavia.

On 9 November 1972 CAAC, which had placed a large number of orders for the smaller Trident 2E, became the second customer (and last) for the Trident 3B when it ordered two longer range versions of the aircraft dubbed the 'Super 3B'. These featured additional centre fuel (the 400 Imp gal tank of the 1E/2E) and gross weight increased to 158,000lb (later increased to 159,900lb). The two Super 3Bs were completed in mid-1975, flying in July and

August that year. The aircraft were delivered to CAAC on 8 September and 17 October, carrying the British marks G-BAJL and G-BAJM, before being registered B-268 and B-270. In 1981 it is thought that the two aircraft were transferred to the Chinese Air Force where they remain in operation.

Although Trident 3B production had now ceased, that of the 2E continued and, in an effort to revive interest in the Trident and extend production, Hawker Siddeley began studies on re-engined twin and trijet versions of the Trident under the project names 'Trident 4 and 5'.

Based around the availability of the so-called 10-tonne engines (either the CFM56 or Pratt and Whitney JT10D), and proposed refanned Spey (the RB163-67 which eventually led to the Tay), Hawker Siddeley proposed four avenues of Trident development which all featured a modified wing: a 3B with two 10-tonne engines; a 3B with extended fuselage (to 140ft 9in) and centre section, powered by two 10-tonners; an extended fuselage twin with a new wing based on A300 technology; and a trijet powered by three refanned Speys and fitted with an extended fuselage (to 153ft 7in) and centre section. The various proposals would have seated between 142 and 180 passengers in mixed class layouts, and effectively meant that Hawker Siddeley had come full circle and returned to the concept of the HS132 'Bident' project of 1965.

By mid-1976 the Trident 4 and 5 plans had been dropped, although the studies led to the European collaborative CAST (Civil Aircraft Study Team) and JET (Jet European Transport) proposals from which the 150-seat Airbus A320 evolved. By now, Hawker Siddeley (soon to merge with BAC and Scottish Aviation to become British Aerospace) had decided upon the 80-seat HS146 feederjet for its future civil programme, production of which was undertaken at Hatfield.

The third and last Trident 3B operator was the Zaïrean airline Air Charter Service (ACS), which acquired five Trident 3Bs from British Airways during 1984, 1985 and 1986, as the airline retired the last of its trijets. The five aircraft were operated on passenger and cargo charter flights on behalf of Zaïrean oil companies, operating mainly in Africa and the Middle East. It is understood that the aircraft did operate with cargo on the main deck, loaded through the narrow passenger doors.

The perils of operating such a sophisticated as well as old aircraft in the depths of Africa do not bear thinking about, particularly considering that the airline probably had very little spares support and even less Trident engineering experience. It seems likely that one by one the aircraft were withdrawn to support those remaining airworthy examples, but by 1988 all the ACS Tridents are thought to have been withdrawn and eventually broken up.

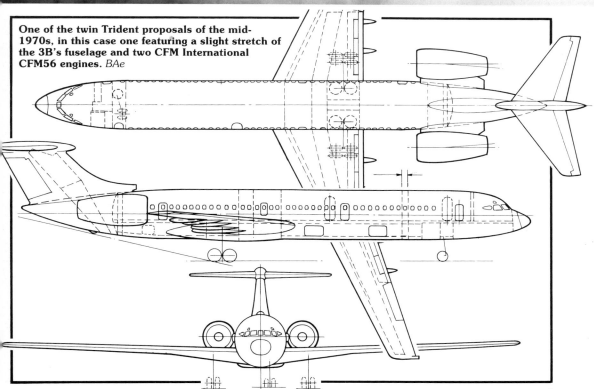

One of the twin Trident proposals of the mid-1970s, in this case one featuring a slight stretch of the 3B's fuselage and two CFM International CFM56 engines. *BAe*

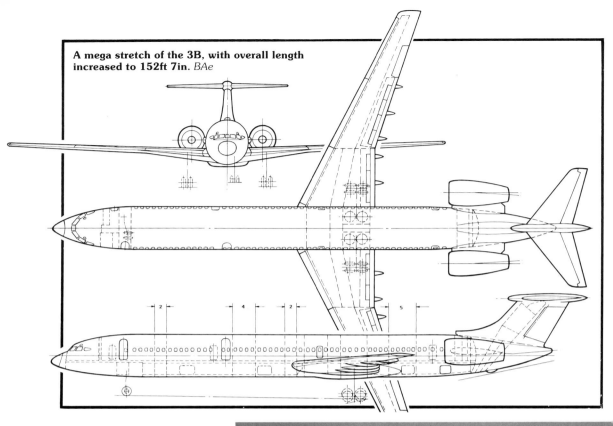

A mega stretch of the 3B, with overall length increased to 152ft 7in. *BAe*

Centre right:
As with many of the Trident 2Es, both CAAC Trident 3Bs were transferred to the Air Force. Here 50058 (ex B-270) takes on passengers through its centre door, whilst a rather unconventional 'air-stair' in the form of a ladder is utilised at the front. *Author's collection*

Bottom right:
Air Charter Service (ACS) of Zaïre purchased five Trident 3s from BA between 1974 and 1986. 9Q-CTY, which incidentally was the incorrect registration, was formerly G-AWZG and is pictured at Heathrow in August 1985. The aircraft was delivered to ACS the following month as 9Q-CTD and was later painted in the airline's all-over white colour scheme. *Peter J. Cooper*

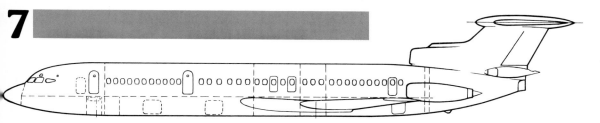

7

Autoland Development

When BEA signed its original contract with de Havilland for the DH121 in 1958, part of the agreement stipulated that 'if, during the service life of the aircraft, automatic landing guidance facilities become available, then additional facilities can be added to provide automatic landing through the autopilot or flight director. It is required that automatic flare-out should be provided from the outset.' As such, the Trident was to be the first airliner to be designed from the start to have the eventual ability to land automatically, enabling it to operate into airports in 'zero zero' weather conditions (zero decision height, zero visibility). During 1958, Smiths Industries was contracted by BEA to develop the Autoland equipment for the new aircraft.

In the late 1950s the only practical experience of automatic landing was held by the Blind Landing Experimental Unit (BLEU) at RAE Bedford where a modified Canberra aircraft was being used to carry

G-ARPB was the backbone airframe of the early Autoland development flying, being used by Hawker Siddeley from 1962-67. Here she is pictured at Hatfield in between tests, wearing the familiar flight-test timing marks on her upper fuselage. *APN*

out automatic landings. The system involved the use of 'Leader Cables' which provided directional guidance and were laid on both sides of the runway, extending several hundred yards beyond the airfield boundary. The programme was aimed at a military rather than civil requirement and, as such, little attention was paid to the redundancy and therefore safety of the system.

A more practical landing aid existed known as 'Instrument Landing System' (ILS), which was a ground based system that transmitted two radio beams, the 'Localiser' and 'Glidepath'. The former was a radio beam transmitted from the end of the runway to give lateral (ie centreline) guidance, the latter being a radio beam transmitted from the side of the runway at 3 degrees to give guidance for the correct angle of descent to the runway. The level of both its low altitude accuracy and its reliability were at the time not considered high enough to allow the safe use of ILS in civil aircraft landing, let alone 'Blind Landing' in low visibility. However, the use of onboard radio altimeters below 150ft to allow automatic flare-outs to be carried out, would overcome the low altitude inaccuracy of the ILS.

'Autoflare' was therefore to become the first phase of the Trident's 'Autoland' ability, with the plan that the aircraft would be introduced into service with this facility. This system, which would be a

Captain's instrument panel (Trident 2). *Kevin Bowen/WTC*

Centre instrument panel (Trident 3). Engine instruments are offset to the right and the large Doppler Moving Map Display dominates. Note the boost engine instrument on the bottom right of the centre panel marked Idle, Flight Idle, Climb, T/O. The large straight lever to the left is the airbrakes control. *Kevin Bowen/WTC*

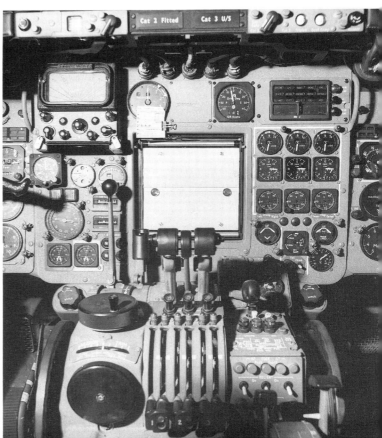

Co-pilot's instrument panel (Trident 2). *Kevin Bowen/WTC*

totally new concept to aircrew, involved the pilot, through the use of the ailerons, keeping the aircraft lined up with the runway whilst the autopilot performed the flare-out. Meanwhile there was a concerted push for the development of more accurate and reliable ILS localiser equipment, improved runway lighting and introduction of a visibility measuring system to enable full-blown Autoland to become a reality.

As the Trident's design was being refined, Smiths had already been working on the Autoland system, the development of which was progressing well. During the late 1950s, modified Vickers Varsities and a de Havilland Comet 2E were allocated to the BLEU at Bedford to assist with the development of automatic ILS coupled approach and landing, using Smiths 'multiplex' autopilot systems.

The multiplex autopilot system involved the use of an autopilot containing multiple sub-channels of control for each axis, each sub-channel being capable of controlling the aircraft and arranged so that in normal use all sub-channels worked together. With a 'duplex' or two-channel arrangement a fault in one sub-channel would be opposed by the other sub-channel and the autopilot would be disconnected, leaving the aircraft in trim for control to be taken over by the pilot. A 'triplex' or three-channel arrangement is designed so that a faulty sub-channel would be outvoted by the other two and then

disconnected, leaving the aircraft still under automatic control at the duplex level.

It was decided that a triplex autopilot fit would be required for the Trident to enable the fully automatic landings that BEA was aiming to introduce into revenue service from 1970 to be carried out. However, it was planned that the Trident would be delivered with a duplex fit from the start to enable the aircraft to have 'autoflare' capability from 1964.

The second Trident to be built, registered G-ARPB, was destined to bear the brunt of the Hawker Siddeley/Smiths Autoland flight testing from 1962 to 1967. After her first flight on 20 May 1962, Papa Bravo initially spent much of her time working on autopilot-coupled approach development — when she was not flying round the northern hemisphere carrying out demonstrations and hot and high trials.

Papa Bravo's early autopilot development work culminated with ARB approval in February 1964 for operation of the Smiths duplex flight system for passenger-carrying use, with the autopilot, flight director, compass and autothrottle being cleared for both enroute and approach use. This enabled the

**Overhead panel (Trident 3).
Hydraulic control levers
(centre) and drop down oxygen
mask covers (left and right).**
Author's collection

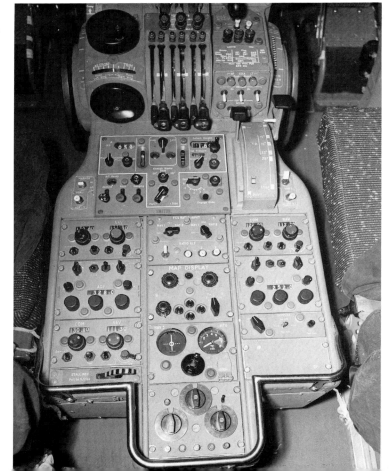

**Centre pedestal, with
flap/droop levers (top right),
engine HP/LP levers (top),
Autopilot controller (centre)
and radio nav/com switches
(left and right). Note also the
large striped lever (bottom
left) — this is the stall
recovery system override
control.** *Kevin Bowen/WTC*

A close-up of the Smiths SEP. 5 Autopilot controller which was located between the two pilots on the centre pedestal. Top left is the Autothrottle control, top centre is the Autoland prime switch and top right is height lock. The three levers (bottom left) were pushed forward to engage the autopilot. *Author's collection*

The Systems Station with instrumentation and controls for the electrical, fuel, hydraulic, pressurisation systems and so on. *Kevin Bowen/WTC*

Trident to enter service the following month with a partial automatic approach capability. By November 1964 progressive assessment of the system had allowed the Tridents to operate coupled approaches down to 150ft, with RVRs of as little as 450yd at certain airfields.

The sophisticated Smiths SEP.5 flight control system which was fitted to the Trident was designed eventually to allow almost all in-flight functions including climb, cruise, descent and the landing, to be controlled automatically. The controller, which was positioned in the centre pedestal between the two pilots, could be primed so that the aircraft would acquire any height, airspeed, Mach number or rate of descent, and it incorporated the autothrottle system. It could also be instructed to assume any of the Trident's navigation systems including compass, VOR and NDB (types of radio navigation beacon), with steering commands displayed on the flight director on the pilots' forward instrument panel.

There was a rather amusing side to all this new automatic technology. Soon after the introduction of the Trident into revenue service, BEA found that inexperienced passengers were being worried by the frequent variations in engine power (and noise) on approach that were a characteristic of the autothrottle system. The airline decided to attach an explanatory note to the passengers' in-flight bulletin to put their minds at rest.

As part of the aircraft's all-weather capability it was planned from the start to equip the Trident's forward instrument panels with 'howgozit' indicators to give information on the progress of the final approach. As part of the Autoland instrumentation the Para Visual Director (PVD) was devised, which was mounted on each pilot's glare shield. The PVD system, which resembled a barber's pole, gave the crew bank and roll-out command guidance.

On 3 March 1964, Papa Bravo carried out the Trident's first duplex automatic landings, completing 10 Autolands in all, including six at RAE Bedford and four at Hatfield. Work was now progressing for the approval of Autoflare clearance at the duplex level, before taking the whole process one step further and obtaining duplex and then triplex Autoland clearance. Papa Bravo was formally delivered to BEA on 30 April, but was immediately leased back to Hawker Siddeley and Smiths for continued Autoland development.

ARB approval of the duplex Autoflare system (in Category 1 conditions) was received on 3 June 1965, and the world's first Autoflare touchdown on a commercial service was made a week later on 10 June by Trident 1C G-ARPR when it arrived at Heathrow from Paris carrying 10 passengers. By this time, Papa Bravo had completed some 600 approaches in the proving of Autoflare and Autoland.

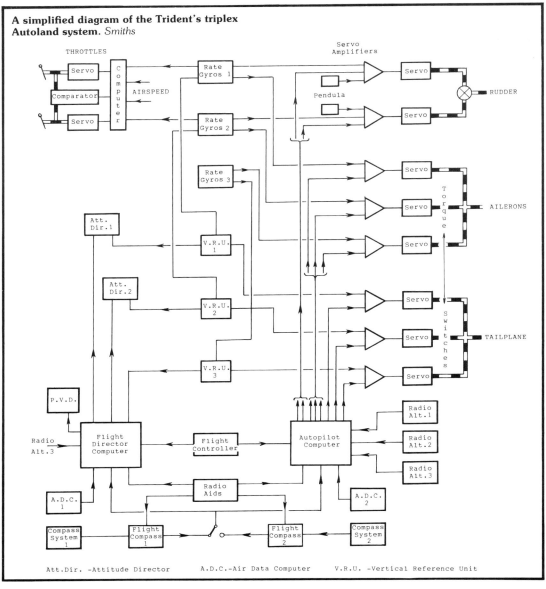

A simplified diagram of the Trident's triplex Autoland system. *Smiths*

Att.Dir. -Attitude Director   A.D.C.-Air Data Computer   V.R.U. -Vertical Reference Unit

G-ARPB was then upgraded with the automatic landing system at triplex level. This featured three sub-channels working together simultaneously on two of the three axes of the autopilot. The likelihood of two parts of the 'triplex' system failing at any one time was extremely remote and therefore gave the necessary reliability and safety. The triplex system gave a safety factor of 10 million to one, somewhat greater than a 'human' pilot and as such it was planned to use the automatic landing capability in fine as well as adverse weather conditions due to the increased accuracy it would provide in the approach and landing phases of flight.

In November 1965, Papa Bravo made its first Autoflares with its triplex Autopilot at Hatfield and, as work continued on the system, the aircraft carried out 15 triplex Autolands at Heathrow on 7-8 September 1966, during two days of demonstrations to world civil aviation heads. By this time she had carried out over 1,500 Autoflares and Autolands including 500 at triplex level.

The following month, on the morning of 4 November, during really foggy weather conditions Papa Bravo made an automatic landing on Heathrow's runway 28L, the first time an airliner had done so at the airport in Category 3B conditions. During the day, three landings were made on two of Heathrow's runways, whilst all other aircraft diverted due to the weather. Papa Bravo then returned to its Hatfield base where it again landed in fog.

Previously as part of the test programme, Papa Bravo had been making automatic landings using the triplex system with the pilot's windscreen blanked off with opaque panels to simulate fog conditions. Of the landings in fog, Hawker Siddeley's Test Pilot Jim Phillips said, 'It was all very relaxing — even more so than practice landings under the hood. All the landings were very smooth and right on the runway centre-line.'

On 24 November, there was more fog in southern England and again no movement was possible at Heathrow, with flights diverted to Luton because of the fog. The opportunity was taken to test the system again in the kind of conditions for which it was designed. This time, a team of engineers and pilots from BEA were on board so that they could

Papa Bravo carried out a number of Autolands in the fog at Heathrow in November 1966. Crew for that first series of Autolands at the airport included (from left to right) Tony Newton (Flight Development Engineer), Ron Jones (Instrument Engineer), Pat Fillingham (Co-Pilot), John Wilson (Chief Operations Engineer), Jim Phillips (Pilot), Jim Crowe (Flight Engineer), Alan Wilmott (Flight Development Engineer) and Rod Ashforth (Smiths Flight Trials Engineer). *Author's collection*

obtain firsthand experience of the system and five take-offs and landings were made in an hour.

In the meantime BEA's Chief Executive, Henry Marking, was returning from Rome, but due to the fog his flight had been diverted to Manchester. As he was due to attend an important meeting of BEA directors in London that evening, it was arranged that G-ARPB should fly to Manchester and bring him to Heathrow, where he was duly landed, in the fog and in the dark, to make the sixth successful automatic landing that day. At the BEA board meeting the following day, the decision was taken to equip its entire Trident fleet with triplex Autoland to enable operations in full Category 3B conditions. The events of 24 November made headlines in the national press, which included 'Trident in first "robot" landing' (*Daily Mirror*) and 'Happy Landings in Fog' (*Daily Express*).

Capt Arthur Johnson, BEA's Trident Flight Manager commented, '(the system) puts us five to 10 years ahead of any other airline in the world. By 1970 BEA will be the only airline anywhere able to keep on operating in the sort of fog we had today. I visualise that we could be the only airline operating anywhere in Europe on a really foggy day.'

On 20 January 1967 the flight development programme for Category 3 automatic landings with Papa Bravo was completed. Starting in May 1965, the programme included more than 2,000 automatic landings at 'duplex' and 'triplex' levels and culminated in a final demonstration of 200 landings

'Look no hands!' Pat Fillingham and Jim Phillips show off their latest trick in Papa Bravo. This was of course for demonstration purposes only — in line service BEA crews were required to shadow the Autopilot's movements with their hands on the controls. *D. M. Stroud collection*

using the standard of equipment which it proposed to certificate for BEA.

Among the advanced facilities demonstrated during the programme were automatic kick-off drift, ground roll guidance during take-off and roll-out, and the ability to overshoot automatically at any height during the approach — right down to ground level — and included simulated engine failure. During the series of 200 landings required for certification, the system was shown to be capable of performing satisfactorily in crosswinds of up to 25kt and in heavy turbulence associated with winds of up to 35kt. These demonstrations were designed to prove to the ARB that the system would perform satisfactorily in Category 3 operations.

Certification of Autoland at duplex level, development of which had involved Papa Bravo since June 1965, was achieved on 19 April 1967, initially in Category 1 conditions. On Tuesday 16 May BEA Trident 1 G-ARPP carried out the first automatic touchdown on a scheduled passenger service when it arrived at Heathrow after a service from Nice. This landing marked the commencement of 'Operation Automatic', which involved Papa Papa making 27 duplex automatic landings during a week of scheduled operations. This programme involved Autolands at 15 airfields in nine countries including Amsterdam, Basle, Brussels, Cologne, Frankfurt, Hanover, Madrid, Milan, Palma, Paris, Rome,

G-ARPB finally joined BEA in December 1967 and was replaced by Trident 2E prototype G-AVFA. 'Sweet FA' as she was known served as the Autoland development hack from April 1968 to May 1969 and completed some 170hr of Category 3 development flying. *Author's collection*

The final Trident to serve as an Autoland flight-test airframe was prototype 3B G-AWYZ. This Trident carried out the final sequence of fully automatic landings at Bedford on 6 March 1972 in adverse weather conditions, clearing the way for Category 3A approval. She was handed over to BEA on 23 March 1972. *BAe*

Stockholm, Venice, Zurich and of course London - Heathrow.

Operation 'Automatic' ended at 12.45pm on Tuesday May 23 when G-ARPP touched down automatically at Heathrow airport after flying from Frankfurt. During the exercise 1,400 passengers were landed automatically and altogether a total of 34.5hrs of flying was logged of which as little as 40 secs/hr on average was under manual control (mainly during take-off).

Papa Bravo was finally delivered to BEA in December 1967 and the airline's Trident 1s were cleared for duplex Category 2 auto approaches on 26 January 1968, with full Category 2 Autoland approval following on 7 February. Triplex Category 2 Autoland operations were cleared in September 1968. By this time BEA had carried out 3,000 Autoflares and 700 Autolands in revenue service and Papa Bravo had flown 600 development hours on Autoflare and Autoland. The intention was then to work towards the achievement of Category 3 clearance through in-service proving.

During her time in Autoland development, Papa Bravo had been crewed by a dedicated team of professionals which included Test Pilots Jim Phillips and Pat Fillingham, Chief Operations Engineer John Wilson and Flight Engineers Alan Wilmott,

Tony Newton, Ron Jones, and Jim Crowe, all of Hawker Siddeley, and Rod Ashforth, Flight Trials Engineer of Smiths Industries.

The first Trident 2E (G-AVFA), which was the first Trident to be equipped with a triplex fit from the start, replaced Papa Bravo as the flight development aircraft and the programme commenced to achieve the ultimate BEA requirement: approval of passenger-carrying landings and take-offs in Category 3 conditions, initially at the Category 3A level. Fox' Alpha — or "Sweet FA" as she was nicknamed by her crew — completed 170hr of Category 3 development flying between April 1968 and May 1969, before being handed over to BEA.

In 1970, the prototype Trident 3 G-AWYZ took over for clearance of Category 3 approval, and her equipment fit included ground roll control, ground roll guidance and ground run monitoring. The ground roll control kept the aircraft on the centre-line from touchdown until 80kts, after which the ground roll guidance system provided steering information for the pilot using the PVD for the remainder of the ground run. The ground run monitor gave data on ground speed and runway distance remaining.

The final flight in the development of the Trident's Autoland system took place on 6 March 1972 when a sequence of fully automatic landings were flown at Bedford by G-AWYZ in adverse weather conditions. This cleared the way for full Category 3A operations for the BEA Trident fleet. Final CAA approval for Category 3A operations was granted in May the same year, but the clearance of the ultimate goal, Category 3B, was not received until 1975.

A typical Trident Autoland involves an autopilot-coupled approach with the localiser being captured at the 8-10 mile point from touchdown. The autothrottle is used for the pod engines with the centre engine set at 11,000 rpm and approach flap is selected (droop would already be down at this stage). At 1,200ft, the gear lever is moved to the 'down' position and 'land' flap selected. The two pilots' mode indicators on the forward instrument panels should show 'THROT, AZM, BEAM, G/P' captions, indicating that all systems are normal. At 1,000ft 'Prime Land' is selected on the autopilot controller on the centre pedestal, where the missed approach height is also dialled in. The blue 'rudder' lights on the glare shield are then checked to have illuminated.

Throughout the approach, any deviation in airspeed is sensed and corrected by a gust compensator which pitches the Trident to maintain constant incidence to the airflow. From 700ft and below the triplex radio altimeters (R) begin to register, and as 300ft (R) is passed, P3 (third pilot) checks the triplex and integrity indicators and depending on the status of the systems, announces either 'Autoland 12ft', 'Autoland 100ft' or 'manual land 100ft'. At 133ft (R) the green progress lights on the coaming illuminate to confirm that the glidepath signal has been disconnected and replaced by attitude control, as the aircraft descends in pitch on memory.

From 100ft above the decision height (DH) the captain would be 'head up' trying to seek visual reference. At 70ft (R), the progress lights go out and the throttles begin to close automatically as the flare begins, with the radio altimeters now controlling pitch. At some point before 12ft (R) (the Cat 3B DH), the captain will make his decision to land, and if no visual reference is received by the DH, then an automatic overshoot will be initiated by disconnecting the autothrottle and selecting full power.

At 12ft (R) the green progress lights come on for a second time and the aircraft enters its 'kick-off drift' and roll-out phase, which involves the correction of drift by the rudder calculated by the radio deviation from the localiser. On touchdown the Captain disconnects the autopilot, pressing the large button on the control column, and eases the stick forward. The No 2 throttle is closed and reverse thrust applied. The autopilot keeps the aircraft on the centreline until 80kt, at which time rudder control is disconnected and the PVD unshutters to give the crew steering commands as they bring the aircraft to a halt. The GRM (ground run monitor) provides runway distance remaining from the moment the main wheels touch down. All the crew have to do now is 'grope' their way through the pea soup to the terminal!

One day in the life of BEA's Trident operations, 30 January 1981, sums up all the effort that went into the Autoland development, for on that day thick fog reduced Heathrow's landings from the then average of 375, to just 107, of which over 80 per cent (88) were Tridents and not a single one was a Boeing.

Weather Minima Measurement Explanation

ICAO definitions:

- *Category 1* : Operation down to a decision height (DH) of 200ft with a visibility of more than 2,600ft
- *Category 2* : Operations down to DHs of between 200ft and 100ft with visibility between 2,600ft and 1,200ft
- *Category 3A*: Operation to and along the runway with an external visibility during the final stage of landing down to 700ft (DH of 65ft)
- *Category 3B* : Operation to and along the runway down to a visibility of 150ft, which is sufficient only for taxi-ing (DH of 12ft)
- *Category 3C* : Operation to and along the runway with no external visibility (no DH)

A particularly dramatic study of Papa Bravo just after she has rotated and climbs away. BAe

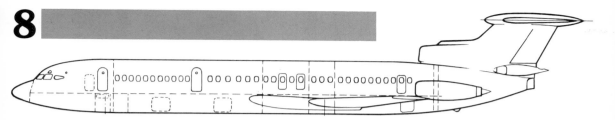

8

In British Airways Service - T-Tales

As is well known, in 1969 the Committee on British Air Transport, presided over by Sir Ronald Edwards (therefore known simply as 'the Edwards Committee'), recommended that the country's two national airlines, BOAC and BEA, should be controlled by a single 'British Airways Board' (BAB). The then Labour government, however, decided to take this one step further and actually merge the two airlines. Thus BAB came into effect on 7 October 1971, and acquired the assets of the two state airlines on 1 April 1972. From this point on the wheels were in motion to create what we all know now as British Airways from two very proud and single-minded airlines. However, the two airlines were not to officially cease to exist until 31 March 1974.

In September 1972, the European Division (ED) of British Airways was credited and BEA began to trade as such 12 months later, with the Trident the mainstay of its fleet. In July 1973 the new British Airways colour scheme was unveiled, taking the best from the existing BEA and BOAC schemes, but as an interim solution, from August 1973 the fleet had their old titles replaced by 'British Airways'. The first Trident to be painted as such was G-ARPU, followed by Trident 2 G-AVFA and 3 G-AWZC. An interesting change was the use of a lower case rather than capital 'T' for the mark of Trident painted on the tail. Fox' Alpha was called upon for an air-to-air photo session resplendent in the new colours. It was to be some years before time was found to paint all the hard working Tridents in the new colours and as such some aircraft ended up looking quite tatty, while others found themselves in some very hybrid schemes.

From 1 April 1973, British Air Services (Northeast/Cambrian) became part of British Airways and

Following the merger of BEA and BOAC, the fleets of both airlines had 'British Airways' titles applied, as Trident 1 G-ARPP photographed at Heathrow in 1975 illustrates. It was to take several years to repaint all the Tridents in the new BA colours and many ended their days in this scheme. *Peter J. Cooper*

the three ex-Northeast 1Es were repainted to carry British Airways titles, before being repainted to wear the full red, white and blue colour scheme. The three 1Es continued to operate the old Northeast services and as such carried small 'Northeast' titles on the forward fuselage. Earlier, in April 1972 Trident 1E, G-AVYD, had been named 'Vicky' by Vicky Leandros, the winner of the 1972 Eurovision Song Contest.

Meanwhile the Channel Islands Division Trident 1E, G-AVYE, was replaced by BAC One-Elevens from November 1973 and so the aircraft joined its three sisters operating the old Northeast routes.

As might be expected, a Trident operated the very last BEA service, BE943 from Dublin to London, on the evening of 31 March 1974. However, it was to be some time before the 'BE' flight number prefix was replaced by 'BA', and the callsign 'Bealine' gave way to 'Speedbird'.

As mentioned elsewhere, in July 1974, two of the Cyprus Airways Tridents leased from British Airways were written off at Nicosia when the Turks invaded Cyprus. The airline's two other Tridents, 1E 5B-DAD (the ex-Kuwait 1E prototype) and 2E 5B-DAC, were eventually returned to British Airways in 1977 after three years interned in Nicosia, taking up their old British marks G-ASWU and G-AVFB.

British Airways introduced Europe's first Shuttle service on 12 January 1975 on the London-Glasgow route with nine specially reconfigured Trident

Some interesting mixes of schemes were applied to Tridents during the 1970s, as the BA paint shop struggled to get all the aircraft into the latest colours. G-AWZJ takes off from Arlanda in 1978 displaying one such variety. *Tommy Lakmaker via John Wegg*

1s. The Shuttle offered hourly services during the week and two-hourly services at the weekend. No booking was required for a guaranteed seat and the regularity of hourly departures was intended to achieve competitive advantage over other modes of transport. To enable all passengers to be guaranteed a seat, a permanent back-up aircraft stood-by at each airport.

The nine Trident 1's standard 109-seat interiors were refurbished at a total cost of £48,000 to seat 100 passengers at a more comfortable 33in seat pitch. The plan was to add 140-seat Trident 3s to the Shuttle fleet when load factors demanded. The Shuttle operation was gradually expanded with Edinburgh being added in April 1976, Belfast in April 1977 and Manchester in April 1979. As the Shuttle established itself, the Trident 3 became the main aircraft allocated to the service, with the Trident 1s and 2s being used as Shuttle back-ups.

Mk 3B G-AWZC was to be the first Trident painted in the new colours. Here she climbs out of Heathrow's runway 28R in 1974. *Peter J. Bish*

Above:
After several years with the Channel Islands Division, from November 1973 Trident 1E G-AVYE joined its three sisters operating the old Northeast routes (note the titles on the forward fuselage). *via John Wegg*

Right:
Still in the old colours, Trident 3 G-AWZZ displays the latest nosewear as she taxies in at Edinburgh. *Author's collection*

Below:
Heathrow during Christmas Day 1977 and no less than 17 Tridents are visible parked on stands and on the crosswind runway. *Peter J. Bish*

Top:
The pilots' favourite, G-ASWU awaits overhaul at Heathrow in 1977. The ex-Kuwaiti Trident 1E joined Cyprus Airways in 1972, but spent three years out of service at Nicosia after the Turks invaded in July 1974. She entered service with BA in 1977 and spent three years with the airline before being withdrawn. *Peter J. Cooper*

Above:
Trident 1C G-ARPH shows off her new BA colours and large 'British' titles that were adopted during 1980. Papa Hotel is now preserved as part of the British Airways collection at Cosford Aerospace Museum. *Author's collection*

By 1975, British Airways had introduced its first 'air buses' into service on its European network in the form of the Lockheed TriStar. This factor, combined with the merger and an economic downturn, saw the airline suffering from overcapacity. During 1974 British Airways made considerable efforts to sell up to 13 of its Trident 1S, particularly in the Far East. Its efforts came to nothing and instead it was

decided to simply retire some Trident 1Cs and seven aircraft were ferried to Prestwick for storage where later they were broken up. Amongst these Trident 1Cs meeting such unceremonious and premature endings was the prototype G-ARPA which was scrapped in early 1976. Additionally one Trident 1C (G-ARPU) was scrapped at Heathrow.

Wing cracks were detected in British Airways Trident 3 G-AWZL in August 1977 during routine maintenance. Part of the problem was thought to be the extremely short sectors these aircraft had been operating, such as on the Shuttle.

The airline's entire Trident 2 and 3 fleets were progressively withdrawn for the repairs to be carried out at Hatfield, Bournemouth and Chester, which took a couple of weeks per aircraft. The repair involved the fitment of armour plating in the areas affected, as well as the replacement of the low drag Kuchemann wingtips with conventional Trident 1-style units. Later the same year, British Airways claimed up to £5.25 million in compensation for the cost of the wing repairs and the loss of revenue that resulted in the aircraft having to be temporarily withdrawn.

T-Tales

For the majority of its time with British Airways when the Trident fleet numbered 60 or 70, there were two separate Flights, with pilots either flying the short fuselage Trident 1s and 2s, or the long fuselage Trident 3s. It was not until the early 1980s when the fleet was down to a small number of mixed variants that the Flights were combined into one and pilots who flew all three variants were labelled 'Tridextrous'.

British Airways pilots who were fortunate enough to fly every variant of Trident were unanimous in their preference from the flying point of view: the Trident 1E was the best and, in particular, the prototype G-ASWU. Unlike the other Tridents in the fleet, the five 1Es the airline acquired were certificated for operation by two pilots and a flight engineer rather than three pilots. Being 'export' Tridents, their flightdecks differed from the BEA machines and lacked the Autoland kit and Doppler moving map display. As such the 1Es were non-standard aircraft.

The prototype 1E G-ASWU joined BA's fleet in 1977, having first served Hawker Siddeley as the development 1E before flying for Kuwait Airways and Cyprus Airways. The aircraft was caught on the ground during the Turkish invasion of Cyprus in 1974 and was ferried back to Heathrow on 12 May 1977. Whisky Uniform served the airline for three years before being scrapped in 1980. During its time with British Airways it even generated its own training manual: 'G-ASWU — the differences'. Also by being a 'Trident one-and-a-half' the aircraft had a higher power-to-weight ratio and different handling qualities to the other aircraft.

The Trident 1C is remembered as being the most 'crisp' Trident to fly although it was admittedly underpowered. With the original 'small, fast wing', the aircraft had a very high cruise speed capability and the original aileron layout allowed for a very high (fighterlike) rate of roll. Some pilots suspected that the Trident 1 could easily have been taken supersonic, although none admit actually trying it!

It is rumoured that a Trident 1 once out-ran some Spanish Air Force F-86s on its way back from Gibraltar. Another Trident once did a beat-up of the flightdeck of aircraft carrier HMS *Ark Royal* whilst base training at Malta.

Capt Colin Rule believes he was on board a Trident for the fastest ever passenger flight from Paris - Le Bourget to Heathrow. On 7 March 1968, Colin (then a Second Officer), Capt Danny Grand and SFO Peter Harper flew G-ARPD from runway 03 at Le Bourget to Heathrow, arriving on runway 05R, completing the journey in a 'chock to chock' time of 27min. Scheduled services to Le Bourget ceased soon after this, and so this record probably still stands.

The longer range Trident 2 had the most powerful engines of the short Tridents but tended to operate at higher weights, therefore negating this advantage. Its long range gave it an extensive route network, operating the longer sectors of the Corporation's network. The 2 was thus a favourite with crews as it enjoyed the more glamorous Mediterranean stop-overs such as Tel Aviv, Athens and Cyprus.

In hindsight most pilots remember the Trident 3 as the most demanding of the bunch to fly. Described by one pilot as 'a bit of a lash-up with its five engines strapped into the tail', the 3s lacked the agility of the original shorter design and were underpowered without the booster, and 'underwinged'. However, when BEA introduced the 3 in 1971, it was the Corporation's 'big ship' and to be transferred on to it was promotion. It also became the mainline Shuttle aircraft in the late 1970s/early 1980s.

The Trident 3B had a change in wing incidence necessitated by the lengthened fuselage which turned it into a different animal on approach, with a much shallower pitch angle. This factor tended to make the aircraft more difficult to land than its short fuselage stablemates, and was therefore more of a challenge.

One landing in a Trident 3 was particularly ropy, with a very high rate of descent over high ground, that the P3 unstrapped himself, stood up, and shouted: 'I completely dissociate myself from this approach!' into the CVR's area microphone (he could have just whispered the same message into his boom mike as it was always live to the CVR).

One Trident 3 captain (who shall remain nameless) had a reputation for being particularly good at demonstrating the Trident 3's hard landing technique. Following the failure of the Vulcans to inflict any significant damage on Port Stanley's runway during the Falklands war, the following spoof notice was displayed on the notice board in the Queen's Building: 'It has been reported that a Trident Three equipped with in-flight refuelling equipment will be flown to the Falklands by Captain "X" where he will use his normal landing technique to crater the runway, and succeed where the V-Force failed'.

The Trident, being an 'economy' aeroplane rather than a 'power' aeroplane like the Corporation's Comet 4Bs, tended to have a hunger for runway length and as such was nicknamed the 'Ground-Gripper' by pilots as it always seemed determined to maintain a grasp on Mother Earth. The aircraft, which some pilots believed relied solely on the curvature of the earth to become airborne, was also susceptible to limitations imposed by air temperature. Ex-Trident Capt Taff Thomas remembers waiting at Istanbul in a Trident 2 for the air temperature to fall. Having preflighted and taxied out, the air temperature had climbed beyond the Trident's WAT limits and so the aircraft taxied back to the ramp. As Ground Control declined to approve a defuel the Trident had to sit patiently and wait for the temperature to fall back within limits again.

During its time with the airline the Trident was also nicknamed 'Tripod' and 'Rodent', the latter being a term of abuse thrown at it by ex-BOAC pilots who transferred to the European Division (ED) to take their command.

Although the Mk 1 was the fastest of all the variants, the other members of the family were certainly no slouches. On a flight back from Scandinavia, the crew of a Trident 3 found themselves witnessing a particularly lovely sunset. A pretty new stewardess who was rather taken by the romantic view, was persuaded to give the skipper a 'good-night kiss' as the red orb dropped below the horizon. She duly complied with the request as dusk turned to night.

However, due to a combination of the high latitude, a very strong tail jetstream and an illegally high mach number, the sun was made to 'rise' slowly above the horizon again and, in awe of the captain's power over the forces of nature, the young lady provided another kiss for him as the sun was going down again!

Although the Gripper's take-off and climb performance could occasionally justify its nickname, former Trident Capt Mike Waldron says that its descent and approach flexibility with the use of airbrake and up to 10,000rpm reverse thrust in the air was legendary. Many a sequencing slot into Heathrow (mainly on to the '10s') could be filled by an approach controller using a pre-Bovingdon or pre-Ockham 'snatch', secure in the knowledge that the Trident with its amazing height and speed loss capability could cope where other aircraft types could not.

So remarkable was the Trident's high speed descent capability that one was once used to demonstrate the sort of rates of descent that an airliner could achieve to some NASA representatives (who included astronauts), when the concept of using reverse thrust on the Space Shuttle was being evaluated.

This capability also allowed Trident pilots to have a reasonably relaxed attitude to descent planning. One very senior co-pilot having endured three days with a keen but obnoxious captain was flying home towards Abbeville in Northern France. His route planning was disturbed by the captain demanding to know if he had calculated his descent point:

'I thought I'd go down at the coast,' came the reply.

'A pre-determined DME was more what I had in mind P2...Anyway which coast are you talking about?'

'Any ****ing coast!' was the reply.

Another nice example of a pedantic captain left with nothing to say on a Trident occurred inbound to Bovingdon in a 3B. Having been told to expect a hold the co-pilot asked for half airbrake to help lose speed in order to establish holding configuration. Although any amount of airbrake could be used, for some reason the Trident 1 had quadrant graduations measured in thirds and the 3 measured in fifths. By now pilots were flying both types. The poor co-pilot was then subjected to a short lecture on this unimportant point by the captain who finally asked 'So how much airbrake do you want?'

'Two-and-a-half fifths please!' came the pert response.

Reverse thrust on two engines in the air was extremely effective but it could leave a bit to be desired when landing a heavy Trident 3 on a short runway. One amusing incident occurred to such a machine one wet and windy evening in Aberdeen.

By the late 1970s the Trident had taken last place behind newly acquired aircraft in the BA fleet and therefore did not experience regular cleaning, shampooing or even painting and as a result the Trident fleet exhibited a distinctly 'used' look. For this evening approach to Aberdeen's short 6,000ft runway 34/16, everything was done by the book — reverse selected in the flare so that it had reached 10,000rpm on touchdown, auto lift-dump primed, maximum reverse thrust after touchdown and maximum anti-skid footbrake.

However, it was apparent that all this was not going to be sufficient to prevent the aircraft from gently aquaplaning off the end of the runway, which it duly did. Having carried out the vital actions and deciding an evacuation was unnecessary, the crew awaited the arrival of the passenger buses while the Trident slowly settled in the mud. The captain's thoughts, a myriad of incident reports and explanations, were suddenly interrupted by the co-pilot: 'At least they'll have to clean and repaint the bloody thing now!'

Incidentally, pilots remember that the Trident's 'Maxaret' anti-skid system never worked properly and high pressure on the pedals could cause tyre bursts in the wet.

Compared with other aircraft the pre-flight checks on the Trident were quite involved. These included the autopilot checks which, in the hands of an 'old stager', looked particularly impressive — engagement and disengagement of azimuth and pitch levers with controlled column pressure and yoke; buttons with subsequent audio warnings; throttle levers moving up and down during the autothrottle checks; disengagement of the Flight Director by manual throttle movement, etc.

These checks could be carried out by one of the front seat pilots. The 'stuck valve check' however needed the co-operation of P3 to make the appropriate hydraulic systems selection (green, yellow, blue) with a lever in a quadrant at floor level behind P2's seat, while the pilot in the front seat performed the appropriate controls lever and switch selection on the roof panel.

One rather self important training captain who was cleared to fly in the righthand seat, dismissed the offer by P3 to make the hydraulic selection and was hoping to impress everyone with his dexterity. All was going well with much hand flashing and lever movement on the roof panel until it was time to make a hydraulic selection. Reaching behind around him with his right hand to move the hydraulic lever in a downward direction from green to yellow, he forgot that the first lever you come to behind the P2 seat was in fact the one used to deploy the Ram Air Turbine (RAT). Situated between the main undercarriage on the underside of the fuselage the RAT duly clamped down with a big clump and hung there much to the surprise of the ground engineer. The result? One red face, two smiles and a 2½hr delay!

When on the ground, Trident crews were required to leave the No 2 engine running until ground power was available, to allow the cabin air-conditioning to operate. On more than one occasion, when the GP took its time arriving, the final shutdown drill could be overlooked. As they left the aircraft, crews would notice what seemed to be an excessively noisy APU. It quickly became apparent that it was in fact the No. 2 engine whirring away at idle, having been accidently left running and the offending pilot would rush back and shut it down!

For this time the Trident was superbly equipped for automatic All-Weather Operations — 12 ft Cat 3B decision height, kick-off drift, gust compensation and GRM (Ground Run Monitor). The latter facility consisted of a reader counter on the forward panel which could be set to the landing distance available and would wind down after touchdown indicating runway distance remaining. A useful instrument in foggy conditions. At other times it was used for a crew sweepstake, 10p a number from 0 to 9, the winner having the correct righthand reader number when the parking brake was applied after arrival on stand. Cabin Crew soon insisted that the indicator was covered to prevent unscrupulous pilots stopping early or late. Chalking initials on the nosewheel tyres was also used as a sweepstake in a similar way, the winner being the one whose name was nearest the ground. In this case flight crews were known to enlist the assistance of the ground engineer to guarantee a win.

One of the Trident's key features was its triplex redundancy in hydraulics, electrics and autopilot. Former Trident Capt John 'Trapper' Holland remembers a particulary hairy moment in a Trident 3 where he was grateful for this redundancy.

In June 1973 John was riding as P3 in Trident 3 G-AWZG when it made a boost-assisted 23 degree

flap take-off from Malta bound for London. Almost immediately after the undercarriage had been retracted the amber 'Electrics' warning illuminated on the CWS and John instantly switched his attention to the systems panel. He realised that the No 1 generator had failed and so brought the APU's generator on line to compensate. However, immediately the No 1 constant speed drive (CSD) temperature registered overheat and almost simultaneously the APU then failed due to low oil pressure. To add to the problems, the flaps had jammed whilst travelling from 23 to 16 degrees.

Obviously a return to Luqa was the only real option, but with its tanks full of fuel for the 3hr trip to London, Zulu Golf was too heavy to attempt a landing immediately. The Trident did not have fuel jettisoning capability and so the crew elected to climb to 8,000ft and fly a holding pattern over the nearby island of Gozo to burn off fuel. To help the fuel on its merry way, the aircraft was flown around with a relatively high thrust setting and full speed brakes. To add to the problems, the No 3 (Blue) hydraulic system also overheated.

The captain, one George Gray, informed the passengers of the situation and told them they had nothing to worry about, suggesting that they sit back, relax and have something to drink. In the event with 16 degrees of flap a smooth landing was made 1½hr later, but when it came to offloading the aircraft it was evident that some of the passengers had taken the captain at his word and were so 'relaxed' that they needed to be helped down the steps! Zulu Golf was AOG (Aircraft On Ground) at Luqa for three days whilst the engineers fixed the problems and the crew were forced to enjoy the 'local facilities' as they waited patiently to fly their Trident home.

It was made known in 1977 that British Airways was considering the acquisition of a number of Boeing 737s (again!) or DC-9s and the 7X7 which was later to become the HS134 lookalike, the 757. In July 1978 British Airways placed a firm order for 19 737-200s and the following month signed a Letter of Intent for 19 757s. The 737 would use around 25 per cent less fuel per passenger than the Trident 3B, whilst the 757 could save between 30-40 per cent depending on the operation.

By the late 1970s, new noise legislation was introduced in Europe which was to dictate the phase-out of the Trident fleet. ICAO Annex 16, Chapter 2 required that all noisy 'Stage 1' aircraft be phased out by the mid-1980s. The Trident was a prominent member of this group and hushkitting had been rejected unlike in the case of the One-Eleven. The Trident's days were therefore numbered. As the legislation was fully defined, it was decided that all British-registered Stage 1 aircraft would have to be phased out by 1 January 1986.

G-AVFB was donated to the Duxford Aviation Society and she is pictured arriving at the airfield during an air day on 13 June 1982. Fox' Bravo, which spent several years with Cyprus Airways, has now been painted in BEA's classic 'Red Square' scheme. *Stephen Matthews*

British Airways began taking delivery of its first 737s in early 1980 and the gradual decline in its Trident fleet began. The used 1Es it had acquired were withdrawn in 1980 and broken up at Heathrow in 1981 including the well-travelled prototype G-ASWU. Trident 1E G-AVYE operated British Airways' last 1E service on 30 September 1980, and was flown to Wroughton in April 1981 to be preserved as part of the Science Museum collection.

More Trident 1s and the first Trident 2s were withdrawn in late 1981, the first four 2s being broken up at Heathrow in 1982. The same year, G-

AVFB was ferried to Duxford for preservation with the Duxford Aviation Society, whilst Trident 1 G-ARPH joined the British Airways collection at Cosford Aerospace Museum. Fox' Bravo has since been restored to her former BEA glory, repainted in the airline's classic 'Red Square' colours of the early 1960s.

During the early 1980s, the Trident found favour with a new employer, the airport fire service, and aircraft were delivered to various UK regional airfields to be used as non-destructive trainers. Far more sinister was the interest that the CAA's Fire Service Training School at Teesside showed in the Trident, had every intention of setting fire to its charges. The first Trident (G-ARPD) was positioned

Trident 1Es G-ASWU and G-AVYC get the axe at Heathrow during 1981. A number of Trident 1Es, 2s and 3s were broken up at the airport during the 1980s. *Author's collection*

to Teesside in August 1981 and, in all, the school has devoured seven Tridents including four 1s, one 2 and two 3s.

When British Airways' Boeing 757 operations began in January 1983, its Trident fleet was down to 36 aircraft, including three 1s, nine 2s and 24 3s. So much slower than the Trident on final approach was the 757 (by around 20kts) that air traffic found that if the former was following the latter, separation had to be increased to 3.5 miles to prevent the Trident being too close inside the outer marker. The arrival of the 757s had further enhanced the airline's 'new generation' fleet and paved the way for Trident 3 withdrawals to commence as well as more 1s and 2s.

The 757, a fine machine in many respects, still found itself being upstaged by the faithful old Gripper. Capt Derek 'Woody' Woodward remembers flying an evening shuttle service up to Manchester with the intention of leaving the Trident at the airport for preservation in the local science museum. The following morning, 757 Shuttle operations from Manchester were supposed to be inaugurated. However, the morning dawned foggy and visibility was outside the 757's operating limits. Therefore Woody and his crew were rapidly called upon to resurrect the Trident, and then proceeded to fly four Category 3 landings at Heathrow and Manchester that day.

Left:
G-ARPZ flew the last British Airways Trident 1C service when it operated a shuttle flight from Glasgow to Heathrow on 2 April 1983. Five days later she was ferried to Dunsfold where she is used by RFD Aviation and now sits on her belly, used for air bag tests. *Richard O. Walker*

Left:
Trident 2 G-AZXM taxies in at Edinburgh during the 1980s. Originally delivered to Cyprus Airways as 5B-DAA, X-ray Mike was swapped for BEA Trident 2 G-AVFB after a hard landing at Nicosia in 1972. *Author's collection*

On the horizon was the enforcement of the ICAO Annex 16 Chapter 2 noise legislation in Europe from 1 January 1986 which would effectively ban all noisy Trident commercial operations in Europe from that date (hushkitting the Trident's three Speys was not considered practicable).

British Airways' last Trident 1C revenue flight took place on 4 April 1983 when G-ARPZ (msn 2128) operated the Shuttle service from Glasgow to Heathrow. The last Trident 1 flight occurred on 12 December 1983 when Capts Colin Rule and Dick Boas ferried G-ARPO to the CAA Fire School at Teesside as 'Speedbird 9614M'. Papa Oscar was then left to the very destructive devices of the firemen and was eventually burnt.

The first Trident 3 (G-AWZA) was withdrawn in late 1983 and six of the variant were broken up at Heathrow during 1984, whilst two others were delivered to fire services.

By early 1985 BA's operational Trident fleet consisted of just three 2s and 15 3s. During the early part of 1985 six 2s were ferried to Southend for immediate scrapping by contractors. The last two Trident 2 positioning flights occurred on 13 February when G-AVFE and 'FO positioned to Belfast and Southend respectively, leaving just G-AVFG to soldier on for two more months.

Fox' Oscar departed Heathrow in the morning, skippered by Capt Colin Rule, ably assisted by SFOs Peter Frisk and Robin Acton. After pausing for a 'clean' 280kt, 100ft flypast of 10L, Fox' Oscar routed via Stansted, where a low pass was made, to Southend. Two beat-ups of Southend's runway were made followed by a particularly brisk landing. As a tug backed Fox' Oscar into the scrapping bay to await the inevitable, her wingtip was graunched across a skip, to the horror of the crew who were still on board. As far as the tug driver was concerned, she was now just 35 tonnes of scrap metal. Fox' Oscar was parked next to the remains of her sister aircraft G-AZXM and G-AVFF, and within a month she herself had been broken up.

Fox' Echo left the same day after lunch for Belfast, with Captain Taff 'Foggy' Thomas and

SFOs Steve 'Cleggy' Lenniston and Dave 'Compo' Hood at the controls. These three pilots spent several months flying together during early 1985 and as such became known as 'the last of the summer wine' after the BBC TV series of the same name. Invariably, the stewardess allocated to flightdeck duty was dubbed 'Nora Batty'.

For this last flight a 280kt, 100ft flypast in clean configuration was again carried out along Heathrow's runway 10L, with 'Cleggy' Lenniston pulling her up into a steep climb-out adjacent to the 'November' stands in salute to Shuttle, the Trident's most recent employer. Fox' Echo was then taken up to her ceiling altitude of 40,000ft before descending down to low level after passing Wallasey on Merseyside. After this the Trident crew co-ordinated with military controllers at RAF Valley in Anglesey for a low level run down the Menai Straits before setting course for Belfast.

On arrival at Belfast, one flypast was completed before her 17,949th and final landing. In all Fox' Echo had completed 29,739hr in the air and is in fact the highest time Trident operated by BEA/British Airways. She was also the Trident that was used by the Queen and Prince Philip for their State visit to Turkey in 1971. Fox' Echo was on chocks at 5pm and each pilot then shut down one engine apiece for the final time. G-AVFE was handed over to the Belfast Airport fire department

Above left:
The Metropolitan Police acquired a Trident 2 airframe (G-AVFK) in 1982 which it reassembled at its Hounslow Heath training ground. It can be seen on the approach to runway 27L at Heathrow and, when first installed, gave a few pilots a shock! *Peter J. Bish*

Left:
Trident 3 G-AWZU flew BA's last international Trident service on 31 December 1985 when it operated an enthusiasts' charter from Amsterdam to LHR. Zulu Uniform was ferried out to Stansted for the airport fire service in March 1986 where she remains today. *Author*

John Dowling and John McIlwham take G-AWZO down for a 'look-see' of Hatfield's runway 24 prior to making her last landing on the same bit of tarmac from which she started her life 14 years earlier. This ferry flight from Heathrow took place on 18 April 1986 and was the last flight of a Trident by a British Airways crew. *BAe*

'Bye-bye Trident': the last Trident departs Heathrow on 17 May 1985, which was also the last time that the type operated in Europe. The aircraft, 9Q-CTZ formerly G-AWZV, was the last of five Trident 3s acquired by ACS and is pictured departing for Zaïre via Ostend. *Author*

and she resides to this day in a quiet corner of the airport.

The last British Airways Trident 2 services were performed by G-AVFG on 25 April 1985. Flown by Taff Thomas, Merve Dacey and Jim Bounden, she left London - Heathrow at 7.17am operating the Shuttle to Edinburgh. After spending the day at Edinburgh as Shuttle back-up, she commenced her return service (BA4863) at 3.12pm. That last historic flight to Heathrow was completed in 55mins, although at the time it was not known that it was in fact the last British Airways Trident 2 operation.

For several months Fox' Golf was held at Heathrow in a 'fit to fly' condition and was used as a ground trainer. On 27 September 1985 she was rolled out resplendent in the new British Airways colour scheme and then spent several years with BA's Ground Operations Training division. During her time there she acquired the nickname 'Spike', reflecting the fact that she was the last Trident left at Heathrow with the aft-mounted, pointed APU installation. 'Spike' may even have qualified for an

equity card as she starred alongside John Cleese as an extra in the film 'A Fish Called Wanda'.

Sadly however, 'Spike' became surplus to requirements and in September 1990 she replaced the old BOAC/BA Comet 4 as Heathrow fire station's training aircraft. G-AVFG now resides by the fuel farm adjacent to the 09L threshold, looking rather tatty and tired, and what was once called 'Comet Corner' is now known as 'Trident Turn'. 'Trident Turn'.

During the remainder of 1985, the Trident 3 fleet was gradually withdrawn and by December just six British Airways Tridents remained in operation. On 15 December, G-AWZU, skippered by Capt Derek Woodward, flew an enthusiasts' charter from Belfast on behalf of the Ulster Aviation Society. The one-hour trip involved a low level flight around the peat bogs of Northern Ireland. Zulu Oscar, flown by Capt Dave 'Bunny' Warren and SFOs Malc Smith and Jerry Higginson, operated an enthusiasts' charter on 29 December which involved some low level cross country flying and fly-bys at Hatfield, Filton, Lyneham and Heathrow.

The last British Airways Trident revenue services were operated on 31 December 1985 on what was to be a busy last New Year's Eve for the Trident, with ICAO's Annex 16, Chapter 2, noise legislation being enforced the next day. The last international scheduled British Airways Trident service took place that morning when G-AWZU substituted for a 757 on BA634 to Copenhagen and the return (BA635), as this was the route on which the type had begun revenue services 22 years earlier. Skippered by Capt John Dowling, accompanied by Capt Peter Hunt and SFOs Frank Epstein and Mervyn Dacey, Zulu Uniform was in fact dragged in at the last minute when the aircraft allocated to the service, G-AWZV, went sick.

British Airways' last scheduled Trident departure from Heathrow occurred later that morning at 11.35am when G-AWZO operated a Manchester shuttle. At the controls were Capt John McIlwham (FTM Tridents) and SFOs Ian Tait and Derek Smee. After arriving at Manchester, Zulu Oscar operated a one-hour enthusiasts' charter up to Liverpool and the Isle of Man, before returning to Manchester to operate one last Shuttle service.

G-AWZU returned from Copenhagen in the early afternoon and operated the Trident's last revenue departure from Heathrow when she took off from 28L for Amsterdam at 3.43pm. She was oper-

ating an enthusiasts' charter (BA9198C) organised by Ian Allan Travel and 'up front' for this service was Capt Brian Walsh and SFOs Bob Owens and Fred Rothwell.

There is some dispute as to British Airways' last ever commercial Trident service. That evening G-AWZO was flying the last Trident Shuttle service to Heathrow having departed Manchester at 6.25pm, whilst G-AWZU was inbound to Heathrow operating the return leg of the charter to Amsterdam. Clearance was received for the two aircraft to formate and the two Tridents flew simultaneous approach and landings to Heathrow, ZU towards 28L, ZO towards 28R.

Although both Tridents landed simultaneously, Zulu Oscar's crew maintain they touched down at 19.08:08, a second after Zulu Uniform and therefore claimed British Airways' last Trident commercial touchdown. What is without doubt is that Zulu Oscar operated the company's last ever scheduled Trident service.

As with the earlier models, several Trident 3s were acquired by airport fire services whilst G-AWZM escaped to the Science Museum Collection at Wroughton (replacing 1E G-AVYE which was later taken to Hatfield and burnt), and the last few aircraft were ferried out of Heathrow in early 1986. The last British Airways-crewed Trident flight was operated on 18 April 1986 when Capts John Dowl-

Three Trident 3s were broken up at Heathrow in June 1986, one of which was G-AWZP. However, the forward fuselage of this aircraft was salvaged for display at the Manchester Museum of Science and Technology. *Author*

The Trident's last stand: British Airways retained two Tridents for several years which it used in the ground training role. Both aircraft were painted in the airline's new colours and, whilst 3B G-AWZK continues in this role, 2E G-AVFG has been transferred to the fire service. *Author*

ing and John McIlwham and SFO Ian Tait ferried G-AWZO for the last time under a 'Speedbird' call-sign to Hatfield for British Aerospace.

During 1984, British Airways sold the first of five 3Bs to Air Charter Services of Zaïre. The first air-craft, 9Q-CTM (ex-G-AWZC), was ferried to Kinshasa in November 1984 and the fifth and last, 9Q-CTZ (ex G-AWZV), on 17 May 1986. The ferry flight of 9Q-CTZ from Heathrow to Kinshasa via Ostend as 'Nine Quebec Charlie Tango Zulu' is thought to have been the Trident's last UK movement. The aircraft took off from Heathrow's runway 10R at 1237 BST, bringing to an end the

Trident era in Europe after some 24 years. One Trident 3 (G-AWZK) was kept at Heathrow and, having been repainted in the new colours, joined 'Spike' in Ground Ops Training, where it continues to be used and is now the last British Airways Trident.

Of the three Trident motion simulators used by BEA and later British Airways at the Heston training centre, only one remains in operational status. The Trident 1 simulator is now preserved (unopera-tional) at Cosford, whilst the Trident 3 ('G-AWZQ') is owned by a private individual and is fully opera-tional. Sadly the Trident 2 unit was left at Heston when the building was demolished, and was broken up.

Fox' Golf, which replaced the Comet 4 at what is now called 'Trident Turn', gets another hosing down from the Heathrow fire service. *Glen L. Palmer*

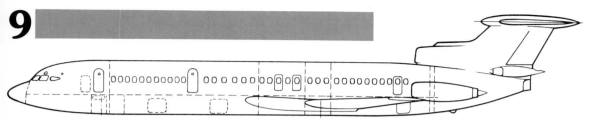

9

The Accidents

Being designed and built by de Havilland, the company that had almost lost everything thanks to the string of accidents that befell the early pioneering Comets, the bottom line in the concept of the Trident was safety. From its triplex redundancy in powerplant, hydraulics, electrics and autopilot, to its strenuous fatigue and systems testing, the Trident featured the ultimate in designed-in safety.

After all the industry debate in the late 1950s regarding how many engines the world's new short haul jets should have, and more importantly their configuration, it is rather paradoxical that the Achilles' heel of nearly all these new short haulers should be their 'T-tailed' layout. Almost universally, the manufacturers decided that the rear fuselage was the best place to put the engines and as a result the horizontal stabiliser was put at the top of the fin.

Fairly early on in flight-testing, it was discovered that the Trident had a tendency not to exhibit the classic nose drop at the stall, but rather pitched up steeply, thereby exacerbating its predicament. The eventual result was what became known as the 'superstall' or 'deepstall', from which recovery was technically not possible.

The Trident was not alone with its deepstall problem, as it was a phenomenon that afflicted all the T-tail jets — in fact the prototype BAC One-Eleven crashed in September 1963 whilst exploring the type's stall characteristics, with the loss of all seven crew on board.

The problems that arose when stalling the T-tailed jets stemmed from the fact that the tailplane was positioned somewhat higher than the main-plane, rather than being directly behind it and therefore safely outside the wing's wake at the stall. As a result, when the wing's angle of attack increased to the point where the air passing over it was no longer 'clean', the tailplane was fed this turbulent, low energy air, which greatly reduced its effectiveness when the pilot commanded a nose down response to recover. To add to this basic problem, the fact that the tailplane was stalled (and therefore no longer providing any significant amount of lift) contributed to the tail-down/pitch-up tendency.

To prevent line pilots from getting into this 'superstall' situation, de Havilland fitted a stick shaker and stick pusher system to the Trident's control columns. The former was a device that rattled the stick to warn that a stall was approaching, whilst the latter incorporated a pneumatic ram that physically pushed the stick forward to lower the nose. The Trident was the first airliner to be certificated with a stick push system.

In September 1964, an *Aviation Week* magazine reporter visited Hatfield to carry out a pilot report on the Trident, during which he was accompanied by Hawker Siddeley divisional test pilot Peter Barlow. During the flight, possibly in light of the concern over the problems of the stalling characteristics, Barlow described the Trident as the 'kiddy car of stallers' explaining that 'you have to be pretty hamfisted to get into (any) trouble'.

Part of the pre-delivery check flying for each Trident involved stalls in various configurations with the protection systems operating, as well as some with the two systems inhibited. At 16.52 on 3 June 1966, Trident 1C G-ARPY, the 23rd BEA Trident off the production line, took off from Hatfield on its first flight, to carry out the first of a series of production test flights under the command of Peter Barlow. The other crew members included George Errington (P2), Edgar Brackstone-Brown ('Brax') (P3) and Charles Patterson (navigator). Papa Yankee was flown out to the northeast and carried out her flight tests over Hawker Siddeley's regular testing ground, East Anglia. At 18.30, the stall tests were commenced and three approaches to the stall were made. With the aircraft in the landing configuration, Papa Yankee's stick shaker operated at 102kt and her stick pusher at 93kt. A fourth landing configuration stall was carried out commencing at a height of 11,600ft but this time, in accordance with the test schedule, the two stall protection systems were inhibited.

As the Trident stalled, she started to pitch down but then the airspeed began to drop off rapidly and the nose down motion ceased, as the aircraft had now entered a deepstall. The nose was seen to pitch up to 30-40 degrees and the aircraft began to turn to port as she descended slowly. The last radio call was received at 18.34 when the crew calmly reported 'we are in a superstall at the moment'. The starboard wing then dropped suddenly and following a short burst of engine power, Papa Yankee began to descend rapidly in a flat spin to starboard, turning once every 6-8secs.

The Trident impacted the ground around 1½min after the stall had commenced, in open farmland about a mile from the Norfolk village of Felthorpe. She hit the ground in a flat attitude with a very high rate of descent but very low airspeed, breaking apart on impact and killing all four crew. A small fire erupted in the area of the No 2 engine but this quickly burnt out. This accident represented the first fatal accident for the type in the four years it had been flying.

Hawker Siddeley and the AIB (Accidents Investigation Branch) immediately launched an investigation, and the official report published two years later concluded that the probable cause of the accident was that 'during the stall test decisive recovery action was delayed too long to prevent the aircraft entering a superstall from which recovery was not possible'.

On 30 June 1966, just 27 days after the Papa Yankee accident, which was in fact the first major incident to befall the Trident, Kuwait Airways' second 1E (9K-ACG) was written off in a non-fatal undershoot at Kuwait Airport. The accident, which happened less than a month after the delivery of the aircraft, occurred during an approach to the airport after a scheduled flight (KU32) from Beirut with 11 crew and 72 passengers on board.

At 20.39 GMT (night) the Trident was beginning its initial approach to Kuwait City, with the aircraft under the control of the autopilot and the requested height of 1,500ft set in the 'height acquire' box. The aircraft turned finals for a visual approach and as 1,500ft was approached, a rate of descent value of 500ft/minute was dialled into the autopilot. However, the autopilot approach was soon abandoned and the handling pilot requested 10,500rpm on all engines. As 700ft was passed the pilot, concerned that his airspeed was now below 150kt, called for 11,500 rpm, but due to his preoccupation with the airspeed, he apparently failed to notice the aircraft's high rate of descent (1,350ft/min).

The co-pilot, who was carrying out his landing checks, noticed through the DV (direct vision or side) window the close proximity to the ground and informed the pilot who then called for 12,000rpm. However, the aircraft struck the ground about 4km from the airport, in an area of soft sand. The impact tore the undercarriage off and the Trident then slid along on its belly for around 1,400ft before coming to rest, badly damaged but substantially complete. Only 11 of the 83 people on board received injuries, and these were minor. Although the aircraft

was immediately reported missing, it took the rescue teams over an hour to find it.

The official cause of the accident was later stated to be due to the high rate of descent and non-observance of company regulations, with corrective action (ie, calling for more power) effectively being too little too late.

Disaster was to strike BEA's Trident fleet at Heathrow on the afternoon of 3 July 1968. That afternoon a BKS Airspeed Ambassador (G-AMAD), operating as a 'flying horsebox', was carrying out a charter from Deauville to Heathrow with eight horses on board. As the aircraft crossed the threshold of Heathrow's northerly runway 28R, adjacent to the ramp of the newly completed Terminal 1, it suddenly veered off the centreline and rolled some 30 degrees to port, careering towards the line-up of BEA aircraft.

At the time BEA Trident 1Cs G-ARPI and G-ARPT were parked empty in front of Terminal 1, being prepared for flights later that day. Having become momentarily airborne again, the Ambassador clipped the tailfin of Papa India with its wing before slicing completely through the rear fuselage of Papa Tango. The aircraft then rolled on to its

The remains of Papa Tango lies scattered across the Terminal 1 ramp after the Trident was struck by a BKS Ambassador. *APN*

What was left of Papa India's tail. Note the APU housing that has been smashed through 90 degrees. *via AIB*

back and smashed into the front of the terminal, killing six of the nine people on the Ambassador, and injuring 28 people on the ground.

The accident investigation found that the accident was caused by the failure, due to metal fatigue, of the actuating rod for the port flap. This had caused the flap to retract, resulting in an asymmetric condition which led to the loss of control of the Ambassador.

Papa India's tail above the 'S'-duct was smashed off, but the damage was deemed repairable and she returned to service the following February, only to crash at Staines three years later. Papa Tango however was so badly damaged that she was later broken up. The loss of these two Tridents, combined with the temporary withdrawal of G-ARPR for repairs following a heavy landing during training at Shannon in June 1968, left BEA suddenly short of Trident capacity. Hawker Siddeley, however, was able to bring forward the delivery of Trident 2s G-AVFC and G-AVFG to assist.

Shortly after take-off from Heathrow on 8 May 1970, the crew of a BEA Trident 2 (G-AVFH) bound for Naples found themselves experiencing a 'stick shaker' stall warning. There was no immediate explanation for this as airspeed and attitude were normal, but suddenly the 'stick pusher' stall recovery system operated pushing the nose down and disconnecting the autopilot. With no immediate reason for the stall evident and height low, the captain overrode the push, bringing the nose back up during which time he just kept the aircraft level, and the Trident 'only just managed to stay flying'.

A second stick push then occurred and as by now Foxtrot Hotel was only 1,000ft above the

On 8 May 1970, Trident 2 G-AVFH came a whisker away from dropping herself all over the local countryside when she stalled shortly after take-off from Heathrow bound for Naples. Papa India was not to be so lucky. *Peter J. Cooper*

ground, the third pilot was instructed to pull the circuit breakers on the rear bulkhead to override the system. As P2 turned to the rear of the centre pedestal to pull the stall recovery override lever he noticed that the droop lever was in the 'up' position and immediately redeployed it.

Although it was established that the droop lever had been moved, no crew member actually remembered moving the lever, and so the captain decided that it had moved as a result of a mechanical failure. Following the incident, Fox' Hotel's controls were comprehensively checked, and no faults were found.

Both BEA and Hawker Siddeley carried out tests to establish what, if anything, had gone wrong with the system, but came up with nothing. It therefore became apparent that there had not in fact been any mechanical malfunction, and it was also established that a similar incident had befallen a Trident shortly after take-off from Paris-Orly a few years before. It was, however, to be another two years before the potential air disasters that had only just been avoided were fully realised.

Sunday, 18 June 1972 was set to go down in British aviation history as the day that the country witnessed its worst air crash. Indeed to this day, the accident that befell the BEA Trident 1 at Staines remains the worst air 'accident' this country has experienced (the Pan Am 747 at Lockerbie in 1988 was as a result of terrorist action).

BEA Trident G-ARPI, one of the airline's 109-seat Mk 1s, was to operate a BEA service (BE548) from Heathrow to Brussels on that wet and blustery afternoon. All 109 seats were taken on the aircraft and, with six crew on board, including pilots Capt Stanley Key and Second Officers Jeremy Keighley

(P2) and Simon Ticehurst (P3), the total number of occupants on the aircraft came to 115.

However, just as the Trident was about to push back from its stand on the Terminal 1 ramp, a three-man Merchantman freighter flightcrew who were needed in Brussels were squeezed on to the aircraft bringing the total number of people onboard to 118. Two of the Merchantman crew members occupied cabin crew seats, whilst the Captain took his place on the flightdeck jumpseat.

At 16.09 Papa India made an apparently normal take-off from Heathrow's runway 28R but just 2½min later, having reached a maximum height of about 1,800ft, she crashed into a field next to the A30 near Staines, Middlesex, killing all 118 on board. The aircraft had hit the ground with a very high rate of descent but very little forward airspeed, having apparently just 'fallen out of the sky'.

The UK AIB found in the subsequent investigation that Papa India's leading edge droop high lift device had been retracted at 162kt Indicated Air Speed (IAS), around 60kt below the safe droop retraction speed of 225kt. As a result the aircraft entered what was known as a 'change of configuration stall', which rapidly led to a 'deep' or 'super' stall, similar to G-ARPY's, from which recovery was not possible. Although the droop retraction was almost certainly executed in error, the exact circum-

The sight that greeted the first rescuers on the scene in the field adjacent to the A30 at Staines that miserable Sunday afternoon. The tail section of G-ARPI came to rest some distance from the rest of the wreckage. *APN*

A general view of the accident site. *via AIB*

The wreckage of G-ARPI was brought to Farnborough and reconstructed, as investigators tried to establish exactly what chain of events led to the accident. The crumpled remains are pictured in the AIB hangar. *AIB*

stances and member of crew responsible were not established.

At the time of the accident, it was not mandatory to equip aircraft with Cockpit Voice Recorders (CVR) and as such G-ARPI was not fitted with one. This made the establishing of the exact circumstances impossible. The Papa India accident has been the subject of many articles and books and still not one conjecture stands out as the most likely scenario on the flightdeck that afternoon.

What is known is that Capt Key was an experienced and much respected (some might say feared) pilot, but also someone who was suffering from a very severe heart condition and should not really have been flying at all. The two co-pilots on the other hand were both very young and inexperienced, particularly 22-year-old Jeremy Keighley who held less than 40hr P2 on the Trident. The ethics of putting two inexperienced pilots together in line operations had been a point of contention for some months before the accident.

It was thought that Key's illness had reached a critical condition during and just after take-off that afternoon, impairing his judgement enough to account for his toleration of speed being low, and could have resulted in him retracting or ordering to retract the droop in mistake for the flaps.

At the time of the accident there was major dispute between BEA and BALPA (British Airline Pilots' Association) regarding pay and working conditions. Some pilots had been favouring strike action whilst others were not, and Key, a firm supporter of the latter, had been canvassing support to avert a strike. During the afternoon of 18 June, he had been involved in a very heated public exchange with a first officer in the crew room over the subject. This outburst itself may have been responsible for the sudden deterioration in Key's condition.

The Trident is fitted with high lift devices on both the leading and trailing edges of its wings, the former being referred to as 'droop', the latter flaps. Unlike other aircraft, the two systems were controlled by a separate rather than a single lever. The sequence of events after take-off called for the flaps to be fully retracted at around 190kt, and the droop at 225kt. Interconnections between the two levers prevented the droop lever being moved whilst any value of flap was selected, eliminating the possibility of mistaken 'up' selections. However, once the flaps were up, the droop lever was unprotected from premature retraction. After the accident, a speed lock was added to the droop lever to prevent it from being moved until a speed of 225kt had been passed, regardless of the flap position.

It was inevitable that in the wake of the public inquiry and investigation that failed to identify the culprit, the press would drag all the crew through the mill. And that they did, tarring Key as an 'ogre' and claiming Keighley was 'sluggish' and 'very inexperienced'. There was even one suggestion that the Merchantman Captain, John Collins, had been spraying air freshener around the cockpit just after take-off, distracting the pilots. A tin of air freshener was found in the wreckage near the cockpit, but this was not unusual as the cans were standard issue to the Merchantman crews as they often carried horses as cargo.

We will never know the truth about what happened on that miserable afternoon, but regardless of whether it was Key or Keighley that inadvertently

Former BKS and Northeast Trident 1E G-AVYD joined BEA's fleet in 1973. Here she is seen on the ramp at Heathrow painted in the new British Airways colours with Northeast titles on the forward fuselage. *APN*

retracted the droop, it was the system as much as the crew that was to blame for the accident. Among the AIB's recommendations following its investigation into the accident were: to fit a baulk to prevent droop being retracted prematurely; to improve pilot training in the area of stall recognition and recovery; to install CVRs; to increase the amount of experience required by young pilots before operating as co-pilots in line service; to improve the ability to detect major heart disease in flightcrews; and to involve the AIB in the investigation of potentially disastrous incidents (such as the Fox' Hotel and Orly incidents).

On the afternoon of 15 September 1975, British Airways Trident G-AVYD, a 1E that had found its way into the airline's fleet through British Air Services (BKS) (which later became Northeast) was operating a scheduled British Airways service (NS552) from Bilbao in Spain to Heathrow with 110 passengers and seven crew on board. The aircraft was taking off from the airport's runway 28 which was very wet with areas of standing water.

As the aircraft accelerated down the runway on take-off, at or about V_1 (decision speed), Yankee Delta encountered one such area of water and a marked deceleration was experienced. The captain elected to abandon the take-off upon which emergency reverse thrust was immediately selected, spoilers deployed and maximum braking applied. It was evident that the aircraft was not going to be brought to a stop on the runway and so the captain

Yankee Delta was damaged beyond economical repair when she overran whilst attempting to abort her take-off at Bilbao in September 1975. Here she is seen awaiting recovery. *AIB*

veered off to the left but as the Trident crossed on to the muddy grass, its right main gear collapsed.

On coming to a halt, the crew operated the engine fire extinguishers and carried out the emergency shut-down drills. All the passengers and crew evacuated the aircraft safely and no significant injuries were reported.

In their efforts to recover the aircraft to render the runway operational, the Spanish authorities managed to inflict even more damage on the aircraft. By the time they were finished the state of the Trident was such that British Airways decided not to repair the aircraft. It therefore remained at Bilbao and was later broken up.

British Airways operated a total of 26 Trident 3s which between them accrued some 560,000hr of trouble-free service with the airline. Twenty-five of the aircraft were retired after serving the airline well for 11-14 years, but sadly one example was to see a premature and horrific end to her days.

On the morning of Friday, 10 September 1976, British Airways' Trident 3B G-AWZT, (msn 2320), was cruising at 33,000ft along airway Upper Blue 1 (UB1) whilst *en route* from Heathrow to Istanbul. She was operating the British Airways scheduled service BE476 with 54 passengers and nine crew on board. Skipper that day was Captain Dennis Tann, with First Officers Brian Helm (P2) and Martin Flint (P3) alongside him.

Zulu Tango's routeing took her through the busy Yugoslavian airspace and in particular over the major 'air junction' at Zagreb. The Trident, callsign Bealine 476, was estimating to cross Zagreb VOR radio beacon (ZAG) at 10.14.

About 25min before Zulu Tango was expected overhead Zagreb, an Inex Adria McDonnell Douglas DC-9 Series 32 (YU-AJR) had taken off from Split in Yugoslavia with five crew and 108 passengers on board operating a German charter flight (JP550) to Cologne. At 10.12, amid some confusion because of overloading in the Zagreb Air Traf-

fic Control Centre that morning, Adria 550 was handed to the upper sector controller, one Gradimir Tasic. As a result of the overloading, the fact that the aircraft was climbing through the Trident's cruising height was not clarified to the contoller. At 10.14:10 this fact was suddenly made very clear to Tasic when the DC-9's crew informed him that they was crossing flight level three two five and estimating Zagreb at one four (10.14).

Tasic suddenly realised that a conflict existed with the Trident, but in his excitement to avert potential disaster he broke into Serbo-Croat, informing the DC-9's crew that there was an aircraft in front of them and to level off immediately. This unfortunate slip prevented the Trident's crew from having any warning of the ensuing danger. By the time the DC-9 had levelled off, it was cruising at exactly FL330 (33,000ft).

As fate would have it, the DC-9 was now travelling from right to left across the Trident's bows at exactly the same height, with the two aircraft closing on each other at around 1,100 mph. At 10.14:41, the outer 15ft of the DC-9's left wing smashed through the forward fuselage and cockpit of the Trident at about window level, killing all three pilots instantly. The Trident then plummeted earthward out of control, spilling some of its contents as it fell. It impacted the ground near the village of Gaj and all 63 people on board were killed.

The DC-9, meanwhile, also went out of control and partially broke up as the remains of its left wing erupted in a fireball and the wreckage impacted the ground in an area some four miles from the Trident. All 113 people on board the DC-9 perished as

Above left:
The remains of Zulu Tango's rear fuselage and tail lie in a field near the village of Gaj. The cylindrical object to the left of the Union Jack is the RB162 boost engine. *AIB*

Left:
The flightdeck came down several hundred feet from the rest of the Trident. Damage caused by the impact of the DC-9's wing is evident. The number '3' is just visible on the nose, which was applied to distinguish between Trident variants. *AIB*

well. A total of 176 people had died that morning apparently as a result of the momentary lapse of the Zagreb ATC.

The official report into the accident determined that improper air traffic control operation was the probable cause. Immediately after the accident, a number of Zagreb's air traffic controllers were arrested and charged with criminal misconduct, with the possibility of 20-year jail sentences if found guilty.

In the end all but one, Gradimir Tasic, were released and later found not guilty. Tasic was left to shoulder all the blame and in May 1977 he was sentenced to seven years' imprisonment. Fortunately appeals were made to have Tasic released, as it was felt that the whole system as much as any individuals were to blame for the disaster. After initially having his jail sentence halved, Tasic was eventually released from prison in November 1978, having served some two years three months.

What is likely to have been the last major accident to befall the Trident occurred to a CAAC-operated Trident 2E on 31 August 1988 at Hong Kong's Kai Tak airport. The Trident (B-2218) was operating a scheduled service (CCA 301) from Guangzhou to Hong Kong with 78 passengers and 11 crew on board. The Trident was being flown by a qualified captain under the supervision of the commander who was acting as co-pilot.

Kai Tak has just one 11,000ft long runway (13/31), most of which is built on land reclaimed from the sea. The northerly end is surrounded by mountains and as such most departures take place using the southeasterly heading runway 13. This departure takes aircraft safely out over the sea between the mountains of mainland Hong Kong and the island of Victoria.

As the Trident commenced its initial approach to Hong Kong (0043 local time), there was a certain amount of heavy rain and cumulonimbus cloud present in the vicinity. 'China 301' was offered and accepted a monitored ILS approach for the airport's westerly runway (31) and the weather reported was as follows: 'Surface wind 090 to 140 degrees at 10kt, heavy showers over the airfield, visibility on runway 31 — 5,000 metres, and on the IGS 3,000 metres'.

The Trident was approaching runway 31 from the east on a heading of 270 degrees at a height of 5,000ft. To facilitate a departure from runway 13, Hong Kong Approach Control intended to vector China 301 through the centreline of 31 and then turn it right to intercept the ILS localiser. As directed, the Trident flew through the centreline, and at 0109 was instructed to execute a right turn on to 360 degrees to establish on the localiser. However China 301 instead requested a left turn to allow it to vector around some 'Cu-Nimbs'. A weather update broadcast shortly after this revealed that the wind had moved round to '120-150 degrees', and it confirmed that the runway surface was wet.

A couple of minutes after its weather avoidance turn, China 301 confirmed that it could accept a 31 approach and the controller saw that the Trident was established on finals. China 301 was cleared for an ILS approach and was informed that it would be PAR (precision radar approach) monitored. China 301 was then instructed to contact Hong Kong Radar, which it did, and a minute after that the controller cleared them to land, although it informed the Trident's crew that he had no precision radar contact.

The Trident was in fact far too low as it approached runway 31's threshold over the sea and its right outboard flaps struck the innermost approach light. Simultaneously the right main landing gear contacted the slope of the sea wall bursting three of the four tyres and tearing the complete unit

plus its support structure from the wing. The Trident now careered along the runway half on its belly and then started to yaw progressively to the right until it was travelling almost sideways, by which time the nose and left main gears had also failed. Its course took it off the runway and across the parallel taxiway and then over the edge of the runway embankment, with it coming to rest in the sea. The fuselage aft the centre door remained above the surface, but forward of this point the airframe broke off and partially sank.

The rescue services were immediately on the scene and a small fire which had started in the area of the No 2 engine intake was extinguished. Most of the passengers were able to evacuate from the aircraft through the emergency exits, but sadly the six flightdeck crew and one passenger in the forward cabin perished.

CAAC Trident 2E B-2218 (ex B-244) is recovered from Hong Kong harbour in August 1988. *AIB*

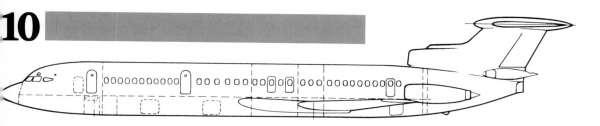

10

Trident to Oslo - From the Flightdeck

'This isn't the regular aeroplane for Oslo?' asked the Norwegian passenger as he boarded British Airways Trident 3 G-AWZJ (msn 2311) one cold lunchtime at Heathrow's Terminal 1 on 6 December 1985. 'No,' replied the stewardess as she directed him to his seat. 'This is a Trident, a lovely old aeroplane which sadly won't be with us much longer.'

She was right. Zulu Juliet was operating British Airways flight BA644 from Heathrow to Oslo, a service normally operated by a Boeing 737. For Zulu Juliet, it was to be her penultimate revenue trip, and for some of the crew as well as Oslo - Fornebu airport, their last Trident service. By the end of the month, all the Trident 3s would be withdrawn, giving way to the airline's Boeing 737s and 757s which had taken over as 'flavour of the month' with British Airways.

The author was fortunate to be flying 'jump seat' on the service to Oslo and back. Zulu Juliet's skipper on that cold and drizzly day was Capt John Villats accompanied by Senior First Officers Paul Heaver and Steve Hurst. Prior to boarding the aircraft, I had joined the crew in the pilot report centre inside the Queen's Building adjacent to Terminal 1 at London - Heathrow, as they ran through the duties and drills for the flight to Oslo.

The Trident is a three-pilot aircraft and for the outbound service Paul was to operate as P2 (ie, co-pilot) and Steve as P3 (flight systems station). They would swap round for the return service.

John checked the weather forecasts, both *en route* and for all destination airports which included Stavanger and Bergen as possible diversions. The Oslo Airfield Briefing Sheet served to remind us that the area around Fornebu airport is particularly noise conscious, although even with the best possible intentions it would be extremely difficult to dis-

guise the arrival, and more particularly the departure, of our Trident 3 that afternoon.

Oslo has limited runway length (for a Trident) and this factor, combined with the weather expected in the Norwegian capital, had led John to plan for a boost-assisted take-off for the return trip. In anticipation of this, he informed the crew that the booster would be employed for the take-off from Heathrow to make sure that all was well with the RB162 for the return trip.

I listened in as John briefed his crew of procedures for the afternoon service. Our flight to Oslo would be by way of a Clacton One Foxtrot SID (standard instrument departure) which involves a climb out towards the north of Heathrow and then east towards the Essex coast and the North Sea. Our initial heading was to be in a westerly direction, as the wind had dictated that the westerly runways were in use. After take-off, our routeing would take us over Colnbrook and, as we passed through 500ft, a right turn on to a northwesterly track of 303 degrees towards Slough and Burnham would be executed, passing to the north of Windsor Castle. At the ATC non-compulsory reporting point TAPLO, which is on the 285 radial, 6 miles DME from the London VOR, another right turn would be made on to a track of 059 degrees towards Chiltern NDB, which must be passed above 4,000ft. A track correction to 069 degrees would then take us over Brookmans Park NDB at 5,000ft, at which time we would change track towards Clacton VOR and the North Sea on a heading of 088 degrees.

It was now time to join the aircraft, which was parked at stand Charlie 28 on the southerly side of Terminal 1's international pier. I bade farewell to the crew as I made my own way to the aircraft.

By the time I had boarded the aircraft, loading was almost complete and the dispatcher was

G-AWZJ taxies out for take-off at Heathrow in mid-1981. Although she still has several years of service left in front of her, her colour scheme is representative of the one she will be retired in.
J. W. Bossenbroek, via John Wegg

putting his finishing touches to the weight and balance sheet. British Airways' Trident 3s were equipped with either 140 or 146 seats, and Zulu Juliet was of the latter configuration. We had 110 passengers on board for the outbound trip, giving us a 75 per cent load factor.

As the scheduled departure time of 1350 GMT approached, Paul called Heathrow Ground for pushback clearance only to be informed that there were single-runway operations and to expect a departure time of 1430. At 1423 pushback was at last approved and once the parking brake had been released, Zulu Juliet lumbered back from the stand with the assistance of her tug. As she did so, the crew lit engines No 2 (centre) and No 1 (left). By the time the ground engineer had disconnected the tug, the crew had completed their start checks and

we were ready to head towards the departure runway, 28 Right (28R).

Ground control directed us to taxi down Heathrow's crosswind runway 23 towards 28R, and we joined the queue waiting to depart, as a stream of aircraft flew in on final approach. As John taxied Zulu Juliet out, Paul ran through the taxi checks, selecting 16 degrees flap and droop, and started No 3 engine. Following a reverse thrust check, Paul started the Boost engine and selected flight idle.

Steve had his P3 seat centred and swivelled forward so that he was facing forward along with the other two pilots. This is standard policy on all Tridents for take-off, climb-out and landing, to enable the crew monitoring system to work. The Trident employs a central warning system (CWS) which is positioned on the centre console within clear view of all three pilots. Any problems with the flight systems that need urgent attention during the critical stages of flight are brought to P3's attention by flashing amber or red lights on the CWS which in turn direct P3 to the relevant panel on the flight systems station.

'Speedbird 644 clear take-off runway 28 right.' Skipper John Willats prepares to take Zulu Juliet into the air. Note the departure procedures chart pinned to the clipboard on the DV window. *Author*

We were at last cleared to line up following a landing Midland DC-9 that had made a particularly hairy approach and touchdown in the blustery conditions. Almost immediately, the Tower cleared us for take-off and Paul applied take-off power and started the stopwatch whilst John held us steady on the centreline. Operational procedure on the Trident required the non-handling pilot to handle the throttle levers during the take-off and the landing. Zulu Juliet began her roll at 1432 GMT and Steve called off the speeds as we rapidly accelerated down the runway: '...100kts...Vee One...Vee R...' John rotated Zulu Juliet's nose up to a pitch attitude of 13 degrees.

Immediately we were airborne and had a positive rate of climb, John called 'undercarriage up', and Paul responded by moving the lever in front of him upwards. The three amber 'undercarriage doors unlocked' and red 'gear unlocked' lights illuminated to indicate that the gear were travelling towards their respective bays, and then they all extinguished, confirming that the wheels were all safely tucked away.

As we pointed skywards and the gear retracted, our surroundings immediately disappeared as we climbed through the murk. Ninety seconds after we had commenced our take-off roll, the engines were throttled back to comply with the noise abatement procedures — the inhabitants below would not have to put up with noisy Tridents for much longer!

At 500ft Paul commenced the 'after take-off' drills. The Azimuth Master switch was engaged bringing up the flight director on both pilots' instrument panels. John continued to fly Zulu Juliet manually towards our initial waypoint, the Burnham VOR. We passed through 2,000ft and our attitude was reduced to around 7 degrees and, as 190kt was passed, Paul retracted the flaps. At 225kt the droop was selected up and shortly afterwards as we accelerated through 235kt, the Booster was shut down. After the aircraft had been 'cleaned up', the autopilot was engaged.

We were transferred to London Control at West Drayton who re-cleared us to continue our climb out, which was taking us over the Chiltern and Brookmans Park NDBs as planned. By the time we reached Clacton we had broken through the cloud which had topped out at 15,000ft and were well on our way to our initial cruising height of flight level (FL) 290 (29,000ft). As Zulu Juliet settled into her Mach 0.80/320kt cruise, Capt Willats briefed the passengers on the flight's progress and informed them that our flight time to Oslo was expected to be 1hr 38min, giving us an ETA of 1710L. The routeing over the North Sea involved crossing pre-planned points derived from cross cuts of radio beacons.

The Trident has a secondary navigation system, Doppler, developed by the Decca Navigator Company and which measures the aircraft's ground speed and drift as well as providing a Distance Gone/Distance To Go function similar to a VOR/DME. The centre instrument panel is dominated by the large square pictorial map display with a pen that displays the aircraft's current position, by way of the Doppler, relative to the airway and way points.

The Doppler along with the sophisticated Smiths Industries SEP.5 Triplex Autopilot effectively make the Trident a 'hands-off' aircraft from moments after take-off to after touchdown should the crew so desire, and despite being some 25 years old in design concedes little in automation technology to its new generation replacements. The crew's role during the cruise is to monitor the automatic systems, as well as to keep a watching eye on engine and control parameters.

'Vee R': Zulu Juliet climbs away at full tilt with her boost engine running (note the open intake door). In this case she is seen climbing away from Schiphol, Amsterdam. *Alan J. Wright*

As I stared out of the port teardrop window at the sun rapidly setting in the west, all I could hear was the rush of air coming over the flightdeck windows. The three noisy Speys that were to be the aircraft's downfall in less than three weeks' time when ICAO Annex 16, Chapter 2, took effect, were only a slight murmur in the background. Indeed, if you asked most Trident passengers about the aircraft's noise problems, they would wonder what all the fuss was about as they sat enjoying the quiet cabin, the entire length of which is situated forward of the engines.

All three of Zulu Juliet's pilots had flown the Trident since they had joined the airline initially flying just the 1s and 2s. Later when the Trident flights were merged, all three pilots were 'Tridexterised', allowing them to fly the 3 as well.

As we neared our descent point, it was now time to tune into Fornebu's ATIS to get the latest weather and runway information. As expected, the 7,200ft long runway 06 was being used for arrivals. We were re-cleared to FL250 and began our initial approach to Oslo.

We descended to FL150 and then down to 80, as we headed towards the Skien radio beacon to the south of Oslo. Situated on high ground at a height of 2,000ft, the ground between the beacon and the airport rose even higher, limiting our minimum altitude to 4,000ft. From Skien we were vectored on to a course of 030 degrees towards Drammen (DRA) which would put us in a position to start our final approach.

As we descended towards DRA we reduced speed to 210kt and Paul extended the leading edge droop, the landing lights swung down and were switched on, illuminating the snow flurry we were flying through. A 'ping...ping' sound indicated the cabin signs had been switched on and 16 degrees of flap was selected. We arrived at DRA at 4,000 ft and were immediately steered on to a heading of 061 degrees for an ILS approach to runway 06. The Trident began its final let down into Oslo, under the guidance of the autopilot, which was now

locked on to the runway 06 localiser and glideslope, and we were fully established on the ILS. As we descended, Paul selected approach flap, gear down and checked three greens and that the nose wheel steering was centred. As we passed the outer marker Paul moved the flap lever to the fully aft position for land flap. The throttles moved forward as the autothrottle commanded additional power and the aircraft trimmed itself for its landing configuration.

As we passed two miles DME from touchdown, a 'clang..clang..clang..' sound indicated that John had disconnected the autopilot. By now the lights of the airport were clearly in sight ahead of us, although all around was darkness. At around 200ft above ground level (the decision height — DH), Paul called 'Decide' to which John replied 'Land' and shortly afterwards commenced the flare. The skipper 'greased' her on and Paul immediately selected 11,000rpm reverse and full wheelbrake was applied.

We turned off the runway at the D5 exit and a 'follow me' van arrived to direct us the short way to our stand at Fornebu's Terminal 1. As we parked, British Airways' local station engineer could be seen waving his arms at us, apparently trying to tell us that our flaps and droop were still down. The levers were already on their way to the up position, which

moments later resulted in a thumbs up from the engineer as the surfaces folded away. Paul shuffled the large tailplane trim wheel forward to set the tailplane angle of incidence fully back, a distinctive characteristic of the Trident when powered down.

Almost immediately, ground power was available and the last of the Speys was allowed to wind down. Our landing time was 1610 GMT or 1710 local (L), and we were 'on chocks' at 1713L, which meant that through no fault of our own we had arrived some 20 minutes later than scheduled. It was John's intention that every effort should be made to ensure that the aircraft was turned around and ready to go back to London as soon as possible, although it was clear that the scheduled departure time of 1745L was beyond reach. Turning the aircraft around in under an hour was however to prove more difficult than anyone envisaged.

The steps were soon put up to the aircraft and our passengers disembarked into the cold Norwegian night for the short walk across the apron to the terminal. The stewardesses were then able to grab a bite to eat before they prepared the cabin for the return flight.

***En route* to Oslo at Mach 0.80.** *Author*

The three pilots stand with their mount in the snow at Fornebu. From left to right: SFO Steve Hurst, Capt John Willats, SFO Paul Heaver and centre, Trident 3 G-AWZJ.
Author

Two of Zulu Juliet's stewardesses grab a bite to eat at the forward Pullman table during the Oslo turnaround.
Author

We were soon joined on the flightdeck by the British Airways station engineer and dispatcher. The former checked with the captain for any faults with the aircraft and the serviceability of the RB162, whilst the latter advised us of our estimated payload for the return trip.

The aircraft was refuelled and restocked in preparation for the return trip and baggage was loaded onboard by the ground staff. Meanwhile Paul, who had now taken up his role as P3 for the return trip, carried out Zulu Juliet's exterior check prior to preparing his calculations for departure and *en route*. Steve tuned in to the ATIS for the latest weather information...'Wind 340 degrees at 6kt. Visibility 10km, cloud two octas at 1,800ft, five octas at 4,000ft, Temperature 4 degrees, Dew Point 10, QNH 1001 Mb'.

Our return service was to be British Airways flight BA645 which translated into the call sign 'Speedbird 645'. Our flying time was estimated at 1hr 44min, although a time of two hours was allocated for the service.

The station engineer remarked to me that he was pleased that John Willats had utilised the booster out of LHR, something some captains might not have had the foresight to do. An unserviceable boost at Oslo in the conditions present would have almost certainly resulted in an AOG situation, with a backup aircraft required if the problem could not have been fixed immediately. The

perils of operating a 14-year-old Trident 3 into frozen Northern Europe!

Passengers began boarding as the dispatcher meanwhile put the finishing touches to his weight and balance sheet. Apparently some passengers were disappointed that they were not to return to London on a nice new Boeing 737 as they had expected, but rather on a dirty old Trident 3.

As the last few passengers were being seated, a problem had been discovered with the number of meals loaded into the galley and a mad search was made to locate additional items. Our scheduled departure time of 1745L came and went as the frustrated flight crew sat helplessly awaiting the completion of the cabin turn around.

As part of his 'control checks', Steve operated the tailplane trim throughout its full range, and then configured it for take-off. At last we were ready to move off at 20min past the hour. John requested start clearance whilst Steve prepared to start the engines. The APU had been left running throughout the stopover to allow the airconditioning packs to remain operational. To start Zulu Juliet's three Speys, Steve switched on the engine start master switch which is located on the roof panel, and the

Zulu Juliet's crew (well most of them) pose in front of Zulu Juliet on what was the type's last service into the Norwegian airport. *Author*

engine selector was moved to the 'No 2' (central) position. The ignition switch which was spring loaded 'off', was switched to 'on' and held for two seconds after which the green ignition lamp illuminated and the green shaft lamp flickered.

As the engine accelerated, the lights extinguished to show all was well. Once the engine had stabilised at 4,500 rpm, the same procedure was carried out to start engine Nos 1 and 3.

Once the three engines were running, Zulu Juliet's positioning at the stand allowed us to taxi straight off without a time consuming pushback. We taxied off the stand at 1820L and care was taken not to swing the left wing into a nearby building as one aircraft had recently done. The taxi out took us on the parallel taxiway across the shorter runway 01/19 to the threshold of the 7,200ft runway 06. During the taxi, Steve set about the start of the RB162, which was a necessity for our imminent departure. The start had to be carried out quite late in the taxi drills, mainly as the selection of reverse thrust, which was a pre-take-off check, would automatically shut the boost down.

Starting the Booster was fairly straightforward and first involved the selection of the Boost Master to 'on' which initiated the opening of the engine's intake doors. These were confirmed open when the green intake light on the roof panel illuminated. The start switch was then moved to start and the green shaft light flickered and then extinguished to confirm a successful start. 'Flight Idle' was then selected and the RB162 promptly spun up as required. An anti-ice check was carried out and everything looked good for our four-engined departure. As we approached the end of the runway, Fornebu tower cleared us to line up for take-off.

At our given take-off weight, the target airspeed for stick rotation (V_r) was some 140kt, with the safe climb out speed around 150kt. The rotate speed was marked on the ASI with a white 'bug'. Once lined up on runway 06, the parking brake was applied as we awaited our take-off clearance. Our departure was soon approved and John applied take-off thrust, as Steve held the aircraft on the brakes. As the thrust stabilised, the brakes were

released and Zulu Juliet lurched forward for take-off.

The ASI seemed to take forever to lift up from its lower stop and register the acceleration that we were experiencing. Gradually the needle crept up to the take-off decision speed (V_1), and then lumbered those extra 40 or so knots to the all important V_r. At last the necessary speed was attained and Steve rotated Zulu Juliet's nose into the climb. Moments later a positive rate of climb had been achieved by which time the red stop bar lights that marked the end of the runway were approaching rapidly. Steve climbed Zulu Juliet at 13 degree pitch attitude.

As the nose gear clunked up into its well just underneath us, the Azimuth Master was engaged bringing up the Flight Director once more on both pilots' instrument panels, and a right turn was commenced on to 170 degrees to intercept the Fornebu 130 radial. This steered us away from the noise conscious city of Oslo, the lights of which could now be seen clearly out to our left.

We had finally became airborne at 1828L and were cleared to an initial height of 3,000ft. We were performing a Skien 1 Alpha SID, that required us, on reaching 3,000ft, to turn on to a heading of 230 degrees towards Groensand beacon and then onwards to Skien. The engines' thrust was then reduced to noise abatement settings, the boost switched to its 'climb' setting, and the flaps were retracted.

Following the noise abatement procedures, Zulu Juliet continued her climb out and, after the droop was retracted, the boost engine was shut down by pushing the 'stop' button on the centre instrument panel. As the engine wound down, the boost master switch was selected 'off' and moments later the intake door light extinguished as the doors snapped closed.

As our Trident 3 accelerated, we established a 320kt climb. With Skien VOR now behind us, we set about our task of reaching our transit cruise height of 31,000ft.

As I chatted to the crew in the quiet relaxed environment of Zulu Juliet's flightdeck, we discussed the technicalities of flying a modern jet airliner, and how automated the 'old girl' was despite her 1960s design roots. Certainly for the crew, the Trident's most outstanding ability was its Autoland capability, which allowed it to 'out-land' BA's more modern 737-200 aircraft when the chips (and the cloud base) were down. It was decided to execute an automatic landing at Heathrow, which would serve as a demonstration for me of how the system operated. The only obstacles would inevitably be the serviceability of the autopilot equipment and the weather conditions.

Our routeing back to Heathrow from Oslo took us on what was effectively the reciprocal of our trip out. After reaching Skien we continued the climb to our cruise height and steered towards the SVA VOR. As with the route out, our way points along Upper Airway 37 for the return were imaginary positions in the North Sea that were located by cross cuts of radials from VORs with DME distances. These were namely DANKO, DANDI, BEENO, and GABBARD.

Our uneventful flight saw us reach 'Gabbard' as scheduled after which we entered the London Terminal Manoeuvring Area. A steering on to a track of 246 degrees pointed us at one last imaginary point, TRIPO, which was some eight miles southwest of Clacton VOR and 35 miles east of Lambourne VOR.

The London - Heathrow ATIS Information 'Romeo' confirmed to us that 28 Right was the arrivals runway and that two-runway operations now existed. Unfortunately the weather information was not good, with three octas (³/₈ths) of cloud at 800ft and a significant amount of rainfall existing. There was also a sporting crosswind of 20kt, which was likely to put paid to any Autoland plans that we had. Fog has never been a problem for the Trident's autopilot, but high crosswinds are a different matter.

London Control cleared us for our initial descent as we steered towards 'Tripo', and then our first real VOR for some time, the Lambourne VOR (115.6 VHF), on a heading of 269 degrees from 'Tripo'. Once past the Braintree South NCATC and 12 miles DME from Lambourne VOR, we were limited to a maximum speed of 250kt. By now we were in contact with Heathrow Approach who had brought our speed back to 210kt and given us further descent clearance. In order to comply with the speed restrictions of the initial approach, the leading edge droop had been deployed.

On arrival at Lambourne, we were slightly surprised that Heathrow Approach instructed us to leave immediately (having expected to be held for at least one orbit), and turned us south towards the ILS intercept point over Central London. Heathrow Director steered us on our southwesterly heading; at the same time an initial 16 degrees of flap was selected. We could already feel the severity of the gale that we had been informed of, which was pitching the aircraft to and fro, but the autopilot was still coping.

We turned finals and intercepted the 28R ILS, the needles on the flight compass and HSI swinging central in unison. We informed Director that we were established and then contacted Heathrow Tower as instructed, and were requested to reduce speed to 180kt and call when passing the Outer Marker. To comply with the new speed restriction, 23 degrees of flap was selected. We were advised of the continuing strong crosswind and rain, and so the planned demonstration Autoland had to be

abandoned. The conditions were such that both the windscreen wipers were running on full song to enable us to see the runway when we went visual.

The gear was selected down and at around the six-mile/1,800ft point, the autopilot was taken out, its disconnect 'clang..clang' adding to the excitement of an already enlivening approach. The conditions were very rough and Steve was battling to keep Zulu Juliet pointing in the general direction of the runway. John informed the Tower that we had passed the Outer Marker and we were cleared to continue. Moments later, Tower cleared us to land and the landing checks were completed, which included the selection of full flap. I tried to make out the approach lights of 28R through the forward windows, and then suddenly spotted them through the right DV window...some crosswind!

The Trident 3 had always been a handful to land, and even a good landing was considered by most pilots as a 'controlled crash'. Steve was about to demonstrate one such arrival, ably assisted by the 20kt gusting crosswind and the harrowing rain. As Zulu Juliet crossed the 28R threshold, Steve 'kicked off' the considerable right drift with the rudder pedals and fought to keep the wings level as the into wind (left) wing tried to rise. We clattered down on to the runway with a thump in true Trident tradition. In the wet conditions, a 'positive' landing was certainly order of the day so as to break through the surface water and avoid the danger of aquaplaning.

Very soon all three sets of wheels had been deposited firmly on the ground and 11,000rpm reverse thrust was bringing us to a shuddering halt. Steve smiled sheepishly but the general feeling was that it had not been as bad as all that, considering the conditions.

We taxied back towards Terminal 1's pier Charlie past the ever increasing lines of British Airways' Boeing 737s and 757s, and nestled neatly into our allocated stand amongst them. We were actually on stand at 1935 GMT, having landed at 1923, some 50min later than scheduled, which served as an illustration as to how lots of niggling little delays can add up, even on relatively short sectors.

Once on stand, the crew switched the wipers off and performed the Trident's shut-down checks. The switch to ground power initially resulted in a second or two of sudden darkness, as the 'juice' failed to come on line at first call. When ground power was finally restored, the APU was shut down. By the time the last of the passengers were leaving the aircraft, the flight crew were also ready to leave.

We all felt that we had experienced a memorable Trident trip as its era with British Airways drew to a close and, although the crew were looking forward to their new challenges, they would always have a soft spot for the 'Gripper'. By the end of December, all the remaining faithful old Tridents had been withdrawn from the British Airways network and the aircraft took up new employment with the various airport fire departments around the British Isles. To the joy of local residents, the days of Heathrow's noisy Trident departures had gone forever.

Zulu Juliet first flew from Hatfield on 9 September 1971 and was delivered to BEA on 16 September. We knew at the time of our flight that her end was near, although we did not realise that she had just one more round trip lined up before her permanent retirement. Zulu Juliet's last service was in fact to be operated three days later on 9 December, to Zurich and back. After a short stay at Heathrow, she departed the airport on 24 February in de-identified form, to take up her new employment as a ground trainer with Prestwick's fire service.

In all Zulu Juliet had completed some 23,118hr and 19,784 landings, giving her an average flight sector length of 1hr 10min. A bit more number crunching reveals that throughout her life she spent an average of 4hr 30min in the air per day, and completed around four flights during each day of her operational life.

As of 1993, Zulu Juliet still resides peacefully at Prestwick airport, being used for non-destructive fire training, during which she is sometimes filled with smoke for forced entry practice. She has been subjected to some unauthorised artistic attention in the form of graffiti applied by students from one of the airport's flying schools. On the right side of the fuselage the numbers '8805' have been applied in large lettering denoting a particular class of the 1988 year. Additionally a large monkey eating a banana has been painted on the tail!

All three of Zulu Juliet's pilots had flown Tridents since they had joined the airline. They all knew that their days flying the type were numbered

as we approached the end of 1985, but only the Captain knew for certain the identity of his new mount. John Willats flew his last Trident service on 30 December, to Amsterdam and back, after which he commenced his BAC One-Eleven conversion course. John, who had joined BEA in 1967 and flown the Trident for 18 years, including five years as a Captain, was to stay with good old British 1960s equipment and the faithful Rolls-Royce Spey engine, at least for the immediate future. In early 1992 he converted on to the Boeing 737.

The destiny of the two first officers was less clear. Paul had one final Trident service scheduled, but this was later cancelled, and so this service to Oslo and back was in fact to be his last Trident sectors. Although he initially had no certain new type immediately lined up, after several months of deliberations and false starts, Paul was eventually to begin a 747 conversion course in May 1986. He continues to fly the airline's -100s and -200s which, with the advent of the all-singing all-dancing two-crew 747-400, have been retrospectively nicknamed the 747 Classic by crews.

Steve, like Paul, had no real idea which type he would be flying next. He flew his last Trident sectors on 20 December, to Amsterdam and back, and eventually joined the British Airtours 737 fleet at Gatwick airport the following March, before switching to One-Elevens a year later. After around three years he switched to the 757, and now flies both that and the 767 on British Airways' international network.

Zulu Juliet as she is today, parked in a quiet corner of Prestwick airport where she is used by the airport fire service for non-destructive training. *Author's collection, via Prestwick Fire Service*

Appendix I — Hawker Siddeley Trident Survivors Listing

As at January 1993

Msn	Variant	Reg	Owner/Operators	Last Service	From/To	Last Flight	Current Status	Location/Base	Remarks
2108	1C	G-ARPH	Cosford Museum	26/03/1982	LHR-GLA	02/04/1982	Preserved	Cosford	Ferried to LHR 26/3/1982. To Cosford 2/4/1982
2111	1C	G-ARPK	Manchester Airport Fire Service	27/03/1982	GLA-LHR	27/03/1982	Retired	Manchester	Ferried to MAN 27/3/1982
2112	1C	G-ARPL	Edinburgh Airport Fire Service	26/03/1982	LHR-EDI	26/03/1982	Retired	Edinburgh	Remained at EDI
2115	1C	G-ARPN	Aberdeen Airport Fire Service	26/03/1982	LHR-GLA	27/03/1982	Retired	Aberdeen	Ferried to ABZ 27/3/1982
2117	1C	G-ARPP	Glasgow Airport Fire Service	23/02/1983	LHR-GLA	23/02/1983	Retired	Glasgow	Remained at GLA
2124	1C	G-ARPX	Air Service Training	23/10/1982	nk	29/11/1982	Instructional	Perth	Ferried LHR-EDI-PRT 29/11/1982
2125	1E	YI-AEA	Iraqi Airways?	01/06/1977	nk-BGW	01/06/1977	Retired	Baghdad?	Probably w/o during war
2127	1E	YI-AEB	Iraqi Airways?	19/04/1977	nk-BGW	19/04/1977	Retired	Baghdad?	Probably w/o during war
2128	1C	G-ARPZ	RFD Ltd	02/04/1983	GLA-LHR	07/04/1983	Experimental	Dunsfold	Flew last BA Trident 1C service. Now sitting on belly
2129	1E	YI-AEC	Iraqi Airways?	08/06/1977	nk-BGW	08/06/1977	Retired	Baghdad?	Probably w/o during war
2130	1E-103	50056	Government of China	-	-	-	Flying	Beijing	
2132	1E-103	50051	Datan Shan Museum	1990?	nk	1990?	Preserved	Nr Beijing	
2133	1E-103	50152	Government of China				Flying	Beijing	
2135	1E-140	4R-ACN	Air Lanka	29/07/1978	nk-CMB	29/07/1978	Instructional	Colombo	Fuselage used for SAS training
2136	1E-110	G-AVYB	Ministry of Defence	31/08/1980	NCL-LHR	31/08/1980	Instructional	Hereford	Last BA 1E service. Ferried to WRT 24/1/1981. Fuse to HAT 22/6/1989
2139	1E-140	G-AVYE	Cabin Sprays	30/09/1980	NCL-LHR	24/04/1981	Experimental	Hatfield	
2141	2E-101	G-AVFB	Duxford Aviation Society	27/03/1985	LHR-MAN	13/06/1982	Preserved	Duxford	Ferried to DUX 13/6/1982. Now in BEA 'red square' scheme
2144	2E-101	G-AVFE	Belfast Airport Fire Service	08/02/1985	GLA-LHR	13/02/1985	Retired	Belfast	Ferried to BFS 13/2/1985
2146	2E-101	G-AVFG	Heathrow Airport Fire Service	25/04/1985	EDI-LHR	25/04/1985	Retired	Heathrow	Flew last BA Trident 2E service. To Heathrow fire service Sept 1990
2147	2E-101	G-AVFH	Mosquito Aircraft Museum	24/10/1981	ABZ-LHR	24/10/1981	Preserved	London Colney	Forward Fuselage to Mosquito Aircraft Museum 13/6/1982
2150	2E-101	G-AVFK	Metropolitan Police	28/12/1981	nk	28/12/1981	Instructional	Hounslow Heath	Fuselage on concrete slabs minus tail and undercarriage
2152	2E-101	G-AVFM	Brunel Technical College	28/11/1983	EDI-LHR	13/01/1984	Instructional	Bristol Lulsgate	Ferried to BRS 13/01/1984
2155	2E-104	5B-DAB	nk	21/07/1974?	nk-NCS	21/07/1974?		Nicosia Airport	Written off 22/7/1974. Substantially complete but derelict
2157	2E-107	B-2201	CAAC	1990?	nk	1990?	Retired	Beijing	
2158	2E-107	B-2202	Air China	Early 1991	nk	Early 1991	Retired	Tianjin	
2160	2E-107	B-2219	CAAC	1990?	nk	1990?	Retired	Guangzhou	
2161	2E-107	B-2223	CAAC	1990?	nk	1990?	Retired	Shenyang	Cannibalised
2162	2E-107	B-2212	CAAC	1987?	nk	1987?	Retired	Shanghai	
2163	2E-107	B-2214	CAAC	1990?	nk	1990?	Retired	Beijing	
2164	2E-107	B-2209	CAAC	1990?	nk	1990?	Retired	Beijing	
2166	2E-107	B-2215	CAAC	1990?	nk	1990?	Retired	Beijing	
2168	2E-107	B-2203	CAAC	1990?	nk	1990?	Retired	Beijing	
2171	2E-108	50052	China United Airlines	-	-	-	Flying	Beijing	
2173	2E-108	B-2213	Museum, Beijing	1990?	nk	1990?	Preserved	Nr Beijing	
2174	2E-108	50158	China United Airlines	-	-	-	Flying	Beijing	
2175	2E-108	B-2204	Air China	Early 1991	nk	Early 1991	Retired	Tianjin	
2176	2E-108	B-2205	CAAC	1990?	nk	1990?	Retired	Shenyang	Cannibalised
2177	2E-108	B-2216	CAAC	1990?	nk	1990?	Retired	Tianjin	
2178	2E-108	B-2210	CAAC	1990?	nk	1990?	Retired	Nanjing	
2179	2E-108	B-2217	CAAC	1990?	nk	1990?	Retired	Guangzhou	
2180	2E-108	B-2211	CAAC	1990?	nk	1990?	Retired	Shanghai	
2181	2E-108	B-2206	Air China	Early 1991	nk	Early 1991	Retired	Tianjin	
2182	2E-108	B-2207	CAAC	1990?	nk	1990?	Retired	Tianjin	
2183	2E-108	B-2220	CAAC	1990?	nk	1990?	Retired	Dalian	Dismantled
2184	2E-108	B-2221	CAAC	1990?	nk	1990?	Retired	Shenyang	Cannibalised

G-AVFG operated the last BA Trident 2 services on 25 April 1985, flown by Taff Thomas, Merve Dacey and Jim Bounden. She was painted in the new colours and used by Ground Ops Training for several years, but is now used by the Heathrow fire service. *Author's collection*

Msn	Variant	Reg	Owner/Operators	Last Service	From/To	Last Flight	Current Status	Location/Base	Remarks
2185	2E-108	50055	China United Airlines	1990?	nk	1990?	Retired	Beijing	Last Trident delivered
2186	2E-108	50054	China United Airlines	-	-	-	Flying	Beijing	
2187	2E-108	50057	China United Airlines	-	-	-	Flying	Beijing	
2188	2E-108	50055	China United Airlines	-	-	-	Flying	Beijing	
2189	2E-108	55053	China United Airlines	-	-	-	Flying	Reigate	Last Trident Built
2310	3B-101	G-AWZI	Surrey Fire Brigade	01/05/1985	GLA-LHR	1/05/1985	Instructional	Reigate	Fuselage to Reigate 28/06/1987
2311	3B-101	G-AWZJ	Prestwick Airport Fire Service	09/12/1985	ZRH-LHR	24/02/1986	Retired	Prestwick	Ferried to PIK 24/02/1986
2312	3B-101	G-AWZK	British Airways	01/11/1985	BFS-LHR	01/11/1985	Instructional	Heathrow	Painted in new BA colours June 1986
2314	3B-101	G-AWZM	Science Museum	13/12/1985	MAN-LHR	28/02/1986	Preserved	Wroughton	Ferried to WRT 28/02/1986
2315	3B-101	G-AWZN	College of Aeronautics	22/12/1985	BFS-LHR	7/03/1986	Instructional	Cranfield	Ferried to CFD 07/03/1986
2316	3B-101	G-AWZO	British Aerospace	31/12/1985	MAN-LHR	18/04/1986	Preserved	Hatfield	Flew last equal BA Trident 3 service. Ferried to HAT 18/4/1986
2317	3B-101	G-AWZP	Manchester Museum of Science	31/10/1985	BFS-LHR	31/10/1985	Preserved	Manchester	Nose section to Manchester Museum 12/06/1986
2318	3B-101	G-AWZR	CAA Fire School	27/09/1985	EDI-LHR	19/03/1986	Retired	Tees-side	Ferried to TSS 19/03/1986. Has now been partially burnt
2319	3B-101	G-AWZS	CAA Fire School	05/12/1985	GLA-LHR	12/03/1986	Retired	Tees-side	Ferried to TSS 12/03/1986. Has now been partially burnt
2321	3B-101	G-AWZU	Stansted Airport Fire Service	31/12/1985	AMS-LHR	5/03/1986	Retired	Stansted	Flew last equal BA Trident 3 service. Ferried to STN 5/03/1986
2324	3B-101	G-AWZX	Gatwick Airport Fire Service	01/10/1984	BFS-LHR	01/10/1984	Retired	Gatwick	Ferried to LGW 1/10/1984
2326	3B-101	G-AWZZ	Birmingham Airport Fire Service	04/11/1984	EDI-LHR	04/11/1984	Retired	Birmingham	Ferried to BHX 4/11/1984
2327	3B-104	50059	China United Airlines	-	-	-	Flying	Beijing	
2328	3B-104	50058	China United Airlines	-	-	-	Flying	Beijing	

The actual status of the Chinese Tridents, both retired and flying, is not really known and therefore unconfirmed

Key to abbreviations

nk — Not Known
ABZ — Aberdeen
AMS — Amsterdam
BFS — Belfast
BGW — Baghdad
BHX — Birmingham
BRS — Bristol Lulsgate
CFD — Cranfield
CMB — Colombo
DUX — Duxford
EDI — Edinburgh
GLA — Glasgow
LGW — London Gatwick
LHR — London Heathrow
MAN — Manchester
NCL — Newcastle
NCS — Nicosia
PIK — Prestwick
PRT — Perth
STN — Stansted
TSS — Teesside
WRT — Wroughton
ZRH — Zurich

Left:
Trident 2 G-AVFH was broken up at Heathrow during 1982, but its forward fuselage is preserved at the Mosquito Aircraft Museum at London Colney, near St Albans. *Author*

Below:
The final line up: the last six Trident 3s await an uncertain future at Heathrow airport in early 1986. From left to right: G-AWZH, 'ZL, 'ZV, 'ZK, 'ZP and 'ZI. *Author*

Appendix II — Tridents Written Off

Date	Msn	Registration	Operator	Variant	Location	No Killed Passengers	No Killed Crew	No On Board Passengers	No On Board Crew
03.06.66	2126	G-ARPY	Hawker Siddeley	1C	Felthorpe, Norfolk	-	4	-	4
30.06.66	2118	9K-ACG	Kuwait Airways	1E	Nr Kuwait City	-	-	72	11
03.07.68	2121	G-ARPT	BEA	1C	Heathrow A/p	-	-	-	-
29.07.69	2120	G-ARPS	BEA	1C	Heathrow A/p	-	-	-	-
12.09/71	2131	256	CAAC	1E	Mongolian Border	-	9	-	9
18.06/72	2109	G-ARPI	BEA	1C	Staines, Middlesex	112	6	112	6
22.07/74	2134	5B-DAE	Cyprus Airways	1E	Nicosia A/p, Cyprus	-	-	-	-
22.07/74	2155	5B-DAB	Cyprus Airways	2E	Nicosia A/p, Cyprus	-	-	-	-
15.09/75	2138	G-AVYD	British Airways	1E	Bilbao A/p, Spain	-	-	110	7
28.12/75	2103	G-ARPC	British Airways	1C	Heathrow A/p	-	-	-	-
10.09/76	2320	G-AWZT	British Airways	3B	Nr Zagreb, Yugoslavia	54	9	54	9
14.03/79	2172	B-274	CAAC	2E	Beijing, China	104	12	-	12
26.04/82	2170	B-266	CAAC	2E	Nr. Guilin, China	104	8	104	8
27.02/83	2167	B-260	CAAC	2E	Fuzhou A/p, China	-	-	96	?
14.09/83	2169	B-264	CAAC	2E	Guilin A/p, China	11	-	100	6
31.08/88	2159	B-2218	CAAC	2E	Kai Tak A/p, Hong Kong	1	6	78	11
22.03/90	2165	B-2208	CAAC	2E	Guilin A/p, China	-	-	102	5

A/p — Airport

Information courtesy of Airclaims Ltd

Appendix III — Trident Variants Specification Chart

Variant	Airco 121	1	1A	1B	1C	1E	1E-110/140	1F	2E	3B	Super 3B
Wingspan	107ft	89ft 10in	104ft	89ft 10in	89ft 10in	95ft	95ft	93ft	98ft	98ft	98ft
Overall Length	126ft 8in	114ft 9in	111ft 9in	114ft 9in	114ft 9in	114ft 9in	114ft 9in	124ft	114ft 9in	131ft 2in	131ft 2in
Height	29ft 1in	27ft	29ft 6in	27ft	27ft	27ft	27ft	28ft 6in	27ft	28ft 3in	28ft 3in
Wing Area	1,920sq ft	1,358sq ft	1,550sq ft	1,358sq ft	1,358sq ft	1,407sq ft	1,407sq ft	1,395sq ft	1,462sq ft	1,493sq ft	1,493sq ft
MTOW	122,500lb	105,000lb	120,000lb	121,500lb	117,300lb	134,000lb	135,580lb	132,000lb	143,500lb	150-155,000lb	159,900lb
Cruising speed	525kt at 25,000ft	511kt at 25,000ft	511kt at 25,000ft	511kt at 25,000ft	511kt at 25,000ft	525kt at 27,000ft	525kt at 27,000ft	516kt at 27,000ft	525kt at 27,000ft	505kt at 25,000ft	505kt at 25,000ft
Typical Range (miles)	1,000	1,000	1,500	2,000	1,150	2,000	2,000	1,300	2,400	1,500	1,900
No of Passengers (Typical)	111	97	79	96	96	103	103	128	103	136	136
(Maximum)		106	100	106	106	139	139	140	139	180	180
Engines	RB 141	Spey Mk 1	Spey Mk 2	Spey Mk 2W	Spey Mk 505F	Spey Mk 511	Spey Mk 511	Spey Mk 512	Spey Mk 512	Spey Mk 512	Spey Mk 512
Static Thrust	12,000lb +	10,100lb	10,680lb	10,680lb	10,050lb	11,400lb	11,400lb	11,400lb	11,960lb	11,960lb	11,960lb
Fuel capacity (Imp Gal)	nk	3,840	4,255	4,840	5,550*	6,000	6,000	5,480	6,400	5,620	6,000
Production years	Not Built	Not Built	Not Built	Not Built	1961-66	1964-69	1968-69	Not Built	1967-78	1969-73	1975
No built					24	10	5		50	26	2

* BEA 1Cs had no centre fuel (ie 3,840 Imp gal)

Mk 1D is believed to have been a short fuselage design for KLM;

Mk 3 was effectively a 3B without the boost engine

During the mid-1980s, the Tridents that had not been transferred to the Air Force were re-registered with four-digit registrations. Thus B-261 became B-2208. The Chinese Tridents' noses were also apparently painted different colours to denote the division of CAAC to which they were allocated. This particular Trident was written off in March 1990 when it overran on landing at Guilin after a flight from Shanghai. *Author's collection*

Appendix IV — Trident Production Allocation

Msn	Variant	Registration	First Flew	Delivered	Operator	Date WFU	Remarks
2101	1C	G-ARPA	09/01/62	18/08/65	BEA	7/2/75	STD Prestwick. BU 4/76
2102	1C	G-ARPB	20/05/62	30/04/64	Hawker Siddeley	1975	LT HS. Ret to BEA 12.67. STD Prestwick. BU 1/85
2103	1C	G-ARPC	25/08/62	09/09/64	BEA	28/12/75	W/O 28/12/1975
2104	1C	G-ARPD	17/01/63	08/01/65	BEA	30/4/81	To Teesside 27/8/81 for Fire School. Burnt
2105	1C	G-ARPE	03/06/63	10/07/64	BEA	1975	STD Prestwick. BU 5/76\\
2106	1C	G-ARPF	18/10/63	19/12/63	BEA	1975	STD Prestwick. BU 5/76
2107	1C	G-ARPG	09/01/64	19/02/64	BEA	1975	STD Prestwick. BU 5/76
2108	1C	G-ARPH	08/03/64	25/03/64	BEA	31/3/75	STD Prestwick. BU 5/76
2109	1C	G-ARPI	14/04/64	02/05/64	BEA	26/3/82	To Cosford Museum 2/4/82
2110	1C	G-ARPJ	01/05/64	26/05/64	BEA	18/6/72	W/O 18/6/1972
2111	1C	G-ARPK	13/06/64	26/06/64	BEA	3/75	STD Prestwick. BU 5/76
2112	1C	G-ARPL	27/07/64	06/08/64	BEA	27/3/82	Manchester Airport Fire Service
2113	1C	G-ARPM	28/09/64	09/10/64	BEA	26/3/82	Edinburgh Airport Fire Service
2114	1E-101	9K-ACF	02/11/64	19/03/66	Kuwait Airways	3/75	STD Prestwick. BU 5/76
2115	1C	G-ARPN	24/11/64	04/12/64	BEA	1/8/80	G-ASWU. To CY reg 5B-DAD. To BA G-ASWU. BU LHR 5/81
2116	1C	G-ARPO	13/01/65	31/01/65	BEA	26/3/82	To Aberdeen 273/82 for Airport Fire Service
2117	1C	G-ARPP	12/02/65	25/02/65	BEA	16/3/83	To Teesside 12/12/83 for Fire School. Burnt.
2118	1E-101	9K-ACG	09/06/65	27/05/66	Kuwait Airways	23/2/83	Glasgow Airport Fire Service
2119	1C	G-ARPR	01/04/65	12/04/65	BEA	30/6/66	G-ASWU. W/O 30/6/1966
2120	1C	G-ARPS	23/05/65	01/06/65	BEA	31/3/81	To Teesside 16/9/81 for Fire School. Burnt.
2121	1C	G-ARPT	30/06/65	09/07/65	BEA	7/69	W/O 29/7/1969
2122	1C	G-ARPU	13/08/65	27/08/65	BEA	7/68	W/O 3/7/1968
2123	1C	G-ARPW	07/10/65	15/10/65	BEA	11/74	STD LHR. BU 11/75
2124	1C	G-ARPX	13/05/66	25/05/66	BEA	26/3/82	To Teesside 26/3/82 for Fire School. Burnt.
2125	1E	YI-AEA	07/09/65	01/10/65	Iraqi Airways	23/10/82	To Perth 29/11/82 for Air Service Training
2126	1C	G-ARPY	03/06/66	—	BEA (not del)	1/6/77	STD Baghdad and poss W/O 91?
2127	1E	YI-AEB	17/02/66	05/03/66	Iraqi Airways	19/4/77	W/O 3/6/1966 on test flight
2128	1C	G-ARPZ	22/06/66	01/07/66	BEA	4/83	STD Baghdad and poss W/O 91?
2129	1E	YI-AEC	27/04/66	13/05/66	Iraqi Airways	8/6/77	To Dunsfold 7/4/83 for RFD
2130	1E-103	AP-ATK	23/11/65	01/03/66	PIA		STD Baghdad and poss W/O 91?
2131	1E-103	AP-ATL	16/03/66	11/04/66	PIA	12/9/71	FF as G-ATNA. To CAAC reg 232. To CAF reg 50056
2132	1E-103	AP-ATM	26/05/66	17/06/66	PIA	1990?	To CAAC reg 256. W/O 12/9/1971
2133	1E-103	AP-AUG	24/08/66	14/02/67	PIA	-	To CAAC reg 236. To CAF reg 50050. Datan Shan Museum
2134	1E-101	9K-ACH	19/10/66	21/12/66	Kuwait Airways	22/7/74	To CAF reg 50152
2135	1E-140	4R-ACN	28/05/69	19/07/69	Air Ceylon	9/7/78	To CY reg 5B-DAE. W/O 22/7/1974
2136	1E-140	G-AVYB	13/02/68	13/05/68	Channel Airways	31/8/80	Reg G-AVYA NTU. STD Colombo
2137	1E-110	G-AVYC	15/01/69	23/01/69	BKS Air Transport	31/07/80	To Northeast 12/71. BU LHR 5/81. Fuse to MOD
2138	1E-110	G-AVYD	17/02/69	05/03/69	BKS Air Transport	15/9/75	BU LHR 4/81
2139	1E-140	G-AVYE	23/04/68	14/06/68	Channel Airways	30/9/80	W/O 15/09/1975
2140	2E-101	G-AVFA	27/07/67	23/12/69	BEA	29/3/83	To BEA 01/72. To Wroughton 24/4/81. BU 6/89
2141	2E-101	G-AVFB	02/11/67	06/06/68	BEA	27/3/82	BU LHR 1/84
2142	2E-101	G-AVFC	03/01/68	06/08/68	BEA	23/10/81	To CY re-reg 5B-DAC. Ret BA G-AVFB. To DAS 13/6/82
2143	2E-101	G-AVFD	15/03/68	16/04/68	BEA	22/3/82	BU LHR 1982
2144	2E-101	G-AVFE	19/04/68	08/05/68	BEA	8/2/85	BU LHR 4/82
2145	2E-101	G-AVFF	14/05/68	30/05/68	BEA	30/11/84	To Belfast 13/2/85 for Airport Fire Service
2146	2E-101	G-AVFG	19/06/68	04/07/68	BEA	25/4/85	To Southend 10/1/85. BU 1/85
2147	2E-101	G-AVFH	17/07/68	01/08/68	BEA	24/10/81	BA Ops Training. To LHR Fire Service 9/90
2148	2E-101	G-AVFI	06/08/68	27/11/68	BEA	11/9/81	BU LHR 5/82. Forward Fuse to Mosquito AC Museum
							BU LHR 5/82